How to Live Without Fear

The Wisdom of Yogananda *series*

How to Live Without Fear

Paramhansa Yogananda

The Wisdom of Yogananda, Volume 11

CRYSTAL CLARITY PUBLISHERS   Commerce, California

© 2024 by Hansa Trust
All rights reserved. Published 2024
Printed in the United States of America

CRYSTAL CLARITY PUBLISHERS
1123 Goodrich Blvd. | Commerce, California
crystalclarity.com | clarity@crystalclarity.com
800.424.1055

ISBN   978-1-56589-346-7 (print)
ISBN   978-1-56589-642-0 (e-book)
Library of Congress Cataloging-in-Publication Data
    LCCN 2023032149 (print) | LCCN 2023032150 (e-book)

Interior layout by Michele Madhavi Molloy
Series cover design by Stephanie Steyer

The *Joy Is Within You* symbol is registered by Ananda Church of
Self-Realization of Nevada County, California.

CONTENTS

INTRODUCTION

Dear Reader:

We welcome you to this new book in the Wisdom of Yogananda series. Here, Yogananda addresses the issue of fear: a highly important topic for all of us.

Very interestingly, Yogananda describes fear — and all other harmful emotions — as mental bacteria. What did he mean by that?

To answer, let's first ask, "What are bacteria"? Bacteria are very tiny single-celled organisms, some of which cause infectious diseases.

In that case, what are "mental bacteria"? They are foreign and harmful mental substances, which enter our psychological structure, making it sick.

Undesired physical bacteria are eliminated by a strong immune system and by specific medicines. Similarly, the mental bacteria of fear can be eliminated by our "immune system" of specific attitudes, and by certain "mental medicines." What are these "medicines"? This is exactly what will be covered in the present book.

The first chapter is dedicated to understanding more clearly how much the mental bacteria of fear conditions our life: fear, anxiety, and worry rob us of our peace, and without inner peace, we can never be happy. Fear poisons the quality of our days, our health, our mental state, our outer success, our entire existence. The more clearly we understand it, the more we will feel determined to eliminate those unhealthy mental bacteria.

From the second chapter onward you will find the specific "medicines" which are "prescribed" to heal your heart and mind of fear.

As always in this series, all sayings, stories, and poems are taken from Yogananda's original lessons, his talks, his magazines (called *East-West* and *Inner Culture*), and also from Swami Kriyananda's work of faithfully recording and sharing his Guru's words.

In Divine Love & Friendship,

Crystal Clarity Publishers

How to Live Without Fear

Chapter One

THE MENTAL BACTERIA OF FEAR AND ITS SYMPTOMS

Fear, worry, and nervousness are mental bacteria which invade the human mind. In India the spiritual "doctors" developed a wonderful system and a science, and a number of unique methods of treating the psychological and spiritual, as well as the physical diseases of man.*

—⟋⟍—

Fear aggravates all our miseries. It intensifies a hundredfold our physical pain and mental agony.

—⟋⟍—

Constant fear affects the heart and may result in palpitation and other heart troubles. Worry and anger affect the brain as well as the whole body and lessen your brain power and general efficiency. So, remember that every time you get angry or afraid, you are causing poison to be secreted in the body. When electric wires in a factory are burnt, they can be replaced by the electrician, but you have been given only one nervous system to carry on the vital functions in the body factory, and if the nerves are burnt up, then you can do nothing to replace them.

* This quote is taken from a newspaper article about Yogananda, quoting his words.

—⟁—

Fear has a very deleterious effect on the heart, nervous system, and brain. It is destructive to mental initiative, courage, judgment, common sense, and to the will.

—⟁—

The digestive organs respond readily, through their connection with the sympathetic nervous system, to mental impressions and therefore, at no time of day do unpleasant impressions do as much harm as at meal time. Anxiety, depression, fear, anger, etc. delay digestion while cheerfulness, hope, courage, and serenity stimulate good digestion. All worry, care, and thought of difficulties should be put aside, particularly while eating and one should always partake of food with a thankful, joyful heart.

—⟁—

Fear of failure or sickness is nourished by thinking constantly of all kinds of dire possibilities, until they take root in the subconscious and finally in the superconscious. Then these fear seeds begin to germinate and fill the conscious mind with fear plants which bear poisonous, death-dealing, fear fruits.

—⟋⟍—

Do not fear accidents and disease because you have recently encountered them. Such fear will create a disease and accident consciousness, and if it is strong enough you will draw to yourself the very things you most fear. On the other hand, fearlessness will in all probability avert them and minimize their power.

—⟋⟍—

Thoughts have materializing power. Beware lest, through fear, you attract the very circumstances which you dread. God is blessing you constantly, but by your doubts you close yourself to His grace, which would dispel your delusions.

Swami Shankara had a woman student who used to come to him all the time with fears and doubts. "What if this should happen?" she would moan, or, "What if I should do that?"

One day this woman said to him, "But — supposing I die?"

Shankara looked at her calmly and said, "All right, then, die!" And the woman fell lifeless to the ground.

It wasn't that Swami Shankara was responsible for her death. He simply allowed her own thought-force to materialize at last, as it would have done much sooner without his blessings. Thus, her soul received a severe lesson, which the guru had been trying in vain to help her to learn by gentler means.

— ⁓ —

The person who is filled with worry and fear has night-mares — which should warn him to change his attitude lest he attract the objects of his worry or fear, not only through his conscious thoughts, but also through the powerful vibrations of his subconscious thoughts.

— ⁓ —

Fear develops in an individual a malignant magnetism by which he attracts the very object of which he is afraid, as a magnet attracts a piece of iron or steel.

—⟋⟍—

You must lose all fear of sickness and accidents; as your body is nothing but energy, it cannot be harmed. When you realize this you will be free.

—⟋⟍—

A mental indulgence in fear will create a subconscious fear habit. Thus, when something really upsetting to the regular routine occurs, the cultivated subconscious fear habit will assert itself, magnifying the object of our fears and paralyzing the will-to-fight-fear faculty of the conscious mind. Man is made in the image of God and has all the powers and potentialities of God; therefore, it is wrong for him to think that trials are greater than his divinity. Remember, no matter how great your trials may be, you are able to conquer them. God will not suffer you to be tempted and tried beyond your strength.

—⟋⟍—

Fear contaminates the emotions with vivid imagination, influencing the subconsciousness to such an extent that it in turn completely destroys the willing efforts of the conscious mind.

—◊—

One of the greatest enemies of will power is fear. Avoid it both in thought and in action. The life force that is flowing steadily through your nerves is squeezed out when the nerves become paralyzed by fear, and thus the whole vitality of the body is lowered. Fear doesn't help you to get away from the object of fear, it only paralyzes your will power. You must be cautious but never afraid. When fear comes the brain discharges the message to all the organs. It paralyzes the heart, disturbs the digestive forces, and causes many physical disturbances.

—◊—

The phenomena of fear is absolutely a mental poison unless it is used as an antidote, a stimulus to spur an individual on to calm caution.

—⟋⟍—

Fear destroys business initiative. It paralyzes the desire to repeat success-producing efforts. Fear eclipses the almighty power of the Soul. Fear nothing else, but try to fear Fear. Be afraid to fear anything else.

—⟋⟍—

Fear throws a veil over intuition and robs you of your confidence to master your difficulties.

—⟋⟍—

If the mind is free from the mental bacteria of anger, worry, fear, etc., and the soul is free from ignorance, no material disease or lack can follow.

—⟋⟍—

Just as songs seem silent and cannot be heard in a room with a broken radio, so through your mind-radio, broken by worries, fear, restlessness, skepticism, or stubborn or chronic sickness, you are unable to catch the health and the power and the wisdom vibrations of God.

—⁓—

Mental disease springs from the invasion of the mental bacteria of fear, worry, anger, dissipation, greed, and bad habits.

—⁓—

Fearlessness is a cardinal virtue.

—⁓—

Prayer

I am protected always,
for the living God goes with me
everywhere on the altar of my
ever-remembering devotion.

The Mouse Who Became a Tiger

A dark forest, inhabited by wild animals, encompassed the holy city of Benares, in India. In the bowels of this deep jungle lay a beautiful Hermitage where lived a great, God-known Saint who possessed many miraculous powers. This holy man had no one near to him in this world except a little pet mouse. Many pilgrims and disciples braved the dangers of ferocious tigers and wild beasts of the forest in order to visit the great Saint, and all brought offerings of fruits and flowers. No disciple ever goes empty handed to his Master, who gives the disciple priceless spiritual treasures. Everyone who came to visit the Saint marveled at the great friendship between him and the mouse, and everybody threw tid-bits to this Sage's pet, who was universally known as the "Saint's Mouse."

One day, when a group of students were visiting the great Master at this secluded Hermitage, they found the mouse being chased by a cat, and he ran squeaking at the feet of the Master Sage for protection. The Sage stopped the cat from its work of crime, and right before the wondering gaze of his students, changed the little trembling mouse into a huge, ferocious cat. The metamorphosed mouse henceforth fearlessly went unmolested in the company of cats. The mouse was happy and only resented it when some of the old disciples would exclaim: "O, look at the Saint's glorified mouse-cat."

One day, while the same group of students were visiting the Master, the cat was being wildly pursued by jungle dogs and came meowing at top speed for protection at the feet of the Sage. The Sage exclaimed: "I am tired of saving you from the vicious dogs. From now on, be thou a wild dog." The disciples were amazed to see the bewilderment and disappointed retirement of the wild dogs, when they suddenly, right before their eyes, saw the mouse-cat change into a dog. The mouse-dog became friendly with the other wild dogs, playing with them and eating the same food with them in a scornful sense of superiority.

On another occasion, while the group of students were studying with the Master, to their utter dismay they found a full-grown Royal Bengal Tiger chasing the mouse-dog, who was racing for shelter at the feet of the Sage. The Master, by his miraculous powers, petrified the tiger, and exclaimed: "Mr. Mouse, I am sick of constantly protecting you from your enemies throughout the day and night, so you must be a tiger henceforth."

No sooner had the Saint said this than the mouse-dog became transformed into a very wild tiger. The students, relieved of their fear, laughed heartily, exclaiming: "Look at that Saint's wild tiger. He is only a glorified mouse." As days went by and the visitors at the Hermitage found out that the fearsome tiger patrolling the place was no other than an uplifted mouse through the miracle of the Saint, often some sarcastic students would be heard saying to newcomers who were afraid of this tiger: "Don't be nervous. That is not a tiger. It is only a mouse glorified into a tiger by the Master."

The mouse who became a tiger got tired of this popular affront constantly hurled at him, so he thought: "If I could only kill the Saint, then the constant memory of my disgrace as his transformed mouse could be removed." Thinking this, the mouse-tiger sprang to try to kill the Sage, to the great consternation of his disciples.

In an instant, beholding the audacious ingrate motive of his transformed pet, the Sage loudly commanded: "Be thou a mouse again," and lo, the roaring tiger was transformed into a squeaking little mouse.

Now, remember, dear friends, most of you forget that by using God-given will power you have changed from a little human mouse, squeaking with failure and fear, into a brave tiger of industry and power, but do not forget that if you try to be antagonistic to that power, you may change again from a tiger of power to a mortal mouse of failure. So, never forget God while you perform your duties, but, no matter what duties you are performing, always in the background of your mind, hum a silent devotional song of love to your beloved Heavenly Father.

—∿—

Chapter Two

HOW TO ELIMINATE THE MENTAL BACTERIA OF FEAR

When you find yourself haunted by fear, the first antidote is to know that you are protected behind the battlements of God's Eternal Safety. Nothing that happens to you can harm your Eternal Self. Even death is but a spiritual anesthetic to relieve one from pain for a period immediately following mortality. Then recognizing fear as an enemy to your sense-to-avert-danger-consciousness:

1. Shift your consciousness to the peace and calmness within.

2. Concentrate upon courage.

3. Summon determination and volition. Will power is the motive power which works the machine of activity.

4. Do something, calmly, and quickly, mustering all the power of your judgment.

5. When fear comes, tense and relax, exhale several times.

———

Switch on the currents of calmness and serenity. Let your whole mental machinery awaken and actively hum with the vibration of will to do something. Then harness the power of will to the cogwheels of fearless caution and continuous good judgment, which in turn must constantly revolve and produce mental devices for escaping your specific impending calamity.

—⁓—

Stand up and tense the whole body — all parts — and then let go. Having done this, you are relaxed. Throw your breath out by forcefully saying, "huh." Do not move.

Tense the whole body again quickly, then let go: throw the breath out again and relax. If your lungs are not in action, every movement is taken away. You are then perfectly relaxed.

Most people when told to relax, keep their muscles contracted. When energy is withdrawn, however, all parts of the body are relaxed and the body is calm.

Close your eyes. Tense the whole body and then relax: there is no greater method of relaxation than the one you are being taught. Any time you are tired or worried, tense and relax the whole body, throw your breath out, and you will become calm. When there is low tensing, tension is not removed, but when you tense high and then relax, you have perfect relaxation.

———◊———

Inhale, then hold the breath and contract the entire body all at once gently. Hold the contraction, counting one to twenty, with deep attention upon the entire body. Then exhale and release the contraction. Repeat three times. Practice any time you feel weak and nervous.

———◊———

Inhaling: contract the body; as you hold: absorb the emotion; then relax: exhaling, and think the nervousness has left you with your relaxation.

———◊———

The *Energization Exercises*, when practiced regularly, will automatically dislodge psychological and spiritual diseases from the inner Self.

———◊———

With closed eyes, concentrate your vision and will in between the eyebrows, and feel the divine memory of all past flowing into you. Pulverize all mental records of accidents, fears, past physical and mental troubles of operations, bereavements, quarrels, depressed experiences, past sinful habits, and thoughts of unkindness of others, or administered hurt by others.

COURAGE

The cure for fear is culturing the consciousness of bravery.

—ᴡᴡ—

Look fear in the face and it will cease to trouble you.

—ᴡᴡ—

Uproot fear from within by forceful concentration on courage — and by shifting your consciousness to the absolute peace within. After you succeed in uprooting fear psychologically, then focus your attention on methods for acquiring prosperity and health.

—◊—

In working out karma, so long as you are still afraid of it you won't yet be completely free.

Karma is best worked out by meeting pleasantly every test that comes, and by accepting courageously any hardship that your tests impose.

—◊—

Kill fear by refusing to be afraid.

—◊—

If you still fear something, that karma has not yet been worked out. To dissipate it, don't try to avoid the tests you have to face. Rise above them bravely, by dwelling in God's joy within.

—◊—

Beneficial changes should be embraced with courage. As long as one's hopes for better things are opposed by fear of their attainment, the mind can never be at peace.

—⁓—

Most people dream at night, but few take their jumbled dreams seriously. So I often say that the greatest lesson dreamland has to offer is that we must not take our earthly experiences too seriously either, for they are nothing but a series of vast dream movies shown to us to entertain us. The Heavenly Father meant to entertain and educate us, His immortal children, with a variety of earthly movies. We must behold comedies, tragedies, and newsreels of life movies, with an entertained joyous attitude, and learn from them without being overcome by their emotional impact.

—⁓—

Resurrect your soul from the dreams of frailties. Resurrect your soul in eternal wisdom. What is the method? It includes many things: relaxation, self-control, right diet, fortitude, an undaunted attitude of mind, regular meditation, and practice of principles. You may fail at first, but do not acknowledge defeat. To acknowledge defeat is greater defeat. You have unlimited power; you must cultivate that power.

Will power and Inner Vigor

A person must be strong-willed to drive away the mind-paralyzing fears and sorrows that would sack and destroy his inner peace. Fiercely — but falsely — they proclaim that the life of the spirit holds no potential for peace or happiness.

—◦◦◦—

When something is threatening to injure you, do not throttle the all-producing inner machine of your consciousness by fear. Rather, use the fear as a stimulus to accelerate your inner machine of consciousness to produce some mental devices which will instantly remove the cause of fear. These mental devices to escape fear are so numerous that they have to be specially fashioned by the almighty tool of consciousness, according to the specific and extraordinary needs of an individual. When something is threatening you, do not sit idle, do something about it calmly mustering all the power of your will and judgment. Will is the motive power which works the machine of activity.

———∿∿———

Nothing could possibly shake my peace or joy, even though the world should collapse. Fear and worry are man's worst enemies, and he can rout these by will if he only tries. The subconscious mind is like a parrot and repeats whatever we tell it; so, instead of suggesting fatigue, complaining, and troubled thoughts to it, suggest joy, opulence, and peace, and these things will be manifested in your life.

———∿∿———

Never allow your courage, or your quick wit in the face of difficulties, to become paralyzed. When unexpected problems overwhelm you with avalanchine force, hie to the divine safety within. Hold aloft the banner of devotion and inner peace, and keep on struggling determinedly until you win through to victory. Never lose touch with your intuitive faith in God; cast about constantly for the slenderest ray of light that might show you the way out of your predicament. God will never let you down, if you firmly hold His hand.

—⚬—

Two Powerful Demands to Be Freed from Fear

1. Demand for Freeing the Mind from Mental Bacteria
   "O Father, Thou art in my mind — I am Thou.
   O Father, Thou art strength:
   Thou art in me — I am strength."

2. Demand to Be Able to Conquer Fear
   Infinite Spirit, teach me to comprehend the utter uselessness of being afraid. Help me to keep in mind that even death, since come it must, at least comes only once and need not be suffered a thousand times, beforehand, through fear! When death does come it will be by Nature's mercy. When it comes, I will welcome it in my soul, for I will understand that it is time for me to move on, lowering the curtain on this life's drama, but traveling, perhaps, to something new and equally interesting. Let me not be a "psychological antique," fearing change.

Teach me not to paralyze my nerves daily with the dread of some future, imaginary accident. Such dread may only invite the accident to happen!

Bless me, that I not let fear anesthetize my mind and shut off my unlimited power, as Thy child, to overcome all tests and trials. Help me to realize that, whether I am awake or asleep, alert or dreaming, Thine all-protecting presence encircles me always.

Help me to see that neither mighty fortress nor the wealth of Croesus could protect me from disease, earthquakes, and all kinds of accidents, that Thou alone art my protector, and that, though I walk where bullets fly or where swarms of bacteria abound, I am ever safe, enhaloed in Thy all-sheltering light.

SELF-ANALYSIS

Now about fear. Analyze a little. Why should you fear? Wisdom only can make you free. Understanding God's law. If I go into a dark room, take a stick and pound the darkness, breaking the table, will the darkness go? No. But if I bring the light in, it goes immediately. Don't be afraid. That won't do any good. Bring in the light of reason. As long as you are not dead, you don't know whether you are going to die or not. When you're dead, it's all over. What's the use of fearing? By fearing, you not only create nervousness, but you move toward the very object of fear.

—※—

Some of the emotions which do most damage are fear, worry, and anger. Fear and worry are closely connected. Worry is usually fear that something undesirable is going to happen which practically never does happen.... A calm analysis of the cause will usually remove the worry. Any violent or continued mental or physical excitement causes a disturbance of the balance in the flow of life-force through the sensory-motor mechanism and the "bulbs" of the senses. It is as if you put a two-thousand-volt current through a fifty-watt lamp. It would burn out the lamp. In the same way, too great a stimulation upsets the functioning of the nervous system.

—※—

Fully analyze what you fear, or what you are excited about. Refuse to accept sudden emotions and excitement. Find the cause of excitement and seek remedy, but do not allow anxiety to rule the mind. Refuse to be obsessed by one idea.

CALMNESS

If you are perfectly calm, you will avoid excitement. If you are too much elated about making money, you will often make wrong speculation or investment. If you are calm, no matter how many propositions people may bring to you, you are always able to separate sentiment from fact. If you fear too much, you bring the very things you wish to avoid. You are destroying vitality of nerves and drawing sickness. When you are full of power and strength and life, it destroys disease. Cultivate peace, calmness, and cheerfulness. The more cheerful and calm you are, the better it is for you. The more you worry or are angry or afraid, the more you are losing poise. The more peace you have, the less nervousness.

—◦◦◦—

How can you obtain poise? If it's difficult to earn money, it is much more difficult to obtain poise. Make a triangle and on one side write SWEETNESS, on the other side write

CALMNESS, and at the base write HAPPINESS; sweetness in speech and mind and body. People have two kinds of nature: the drawing room nature and the home nature. The home nature is when we feel that we are natural but we wish sometimes that we are not natural because in our naturalness we express ugliness. Many people go out all dressed up, but inside passions are boiling and raging within. Inside the house they say, "I am angry." Outside, "Oh, how are you?" Be calm in speech, in mind; be calm in your triune unity. What you *think* you must testify; what you think and speak, your body, soul, and mind, everything must testify. We must have unity of mind, speech, and body. Attain calmness; attain peace; attain happiness; attain poise.

—⚋—

Every night before going to bed, say this: "I am the Prince of Peace sitting on the throne of Poise." Poise is your center. Whether you act quick or slow, you will never lose your kingly attitude of peace. Jesus, Son of God, is the prototype. On Sundays people get religious. One day is better than none, better than nothing at all. But every day ought to be God's day with us. Christ has given us a great ideal that we may live the life of Christ. "To all those who receive Him He gave the power to be Sons of God." Everywhere Jesus demonstrated peace. He passed through all situations, but he had poise and peace. Jesus demonstrated peace in his speech, mind, and body.

———〰———

For ordinary nervousness, take a cold shower or bath. Splash your face with cold water. Partial fasting is good, to go without breakfast or lunch. Keep company with cool, calm people.

———〰———

Be careful in the choice of company. Keep company with people who are calm, strong and wise, with a deeper nature than you have. When a criminal is put into the company of a greater criminal, that does not help him. When it is time for him to leave, the warden says, "When are you coming back?" When nervous people are in the company of other nervous people, they cannot get better. Always choose calm company. If nervous, mix with those who are not nervous.

—⚬—

Always act calmly, be calm in everything; be calmly active and actively calm; have a good diet, but above all move in the company of calm people. Get away from the city once in a while. Above all, remember that you should learn the method of controlling energy. You can contact Cosmic Energy and bring energy into your body, not through imagination. Your body is like a little bubble of energy in the Cosmic Energy; God is everywhere. He controls planets, stars, everything that you see, and yet He is not disturbed. He is above this world, yet He is in this world. You must reflect the image and likeness of God.

—⚬—

Fear should not produce mental inertia, paralysis, or despondency; instead, it should spur you on to calm, cautious activity, avoiding equally rashness and timidity.

—⚬—

Let the screaming hordes of worry surround the ramparts of your inner peace; and let triumphant cries of success invite you to a victory dance when things go well: Remain ever calmly centered in the Self, within.

———

Calmness is another divine experience. This aspect of God is more dynamic and more powerful than that of Peace. Calmness gives the devotee power to overcome all the obstacles in his life. Even in human affairs, the person who can remain calm under all circumstances is invincible.

———

Accept with unruffled mind whatever comes. I often say, "What comes of itself, let it come." This is just as true for the bad things in life as for the good. Only calmness will give you a sense of correct proportion. It will inspire you to behave with unfailing good sense.

DESIRELESSNESS AND NON-ATTACHMENT

Consider the negative aspect of desire. It keeps you forever fearful. "What if this happens?" you think; or, "What if that doesn't happen?" You live in a state of anxiety for the future, or of regret for the past.

Non-attachment, on the other hand, helps you to live perpetually in a state of inner freedom and happiness.

—◊◊◊—

We should strive for health, prosperity, and wisdom without being afraid of failure.

—◊◊◊—

If you have health, but are attached to it, you will always be afraid of losing it. And if you fear that loss, but become ill, you will suffer. Why not remain forever joyful in the Self?

FEARLESSNESS TOWARD DEATH

Another form of fear is the fear of death. Death should be regarded as a universal experience, a change which everyone passes through. It should be looked upon as a good, as a new opportunity, as a rest from the weary struggle on this earth.

When you have made a mess of life, God sends this relief and gives you a fresh trial. Besides, there is nothing to fear, because as long as you are not dead, you are alive, and when you are dead, it is all over and there is nothing then to worry about.

This fear is born of the greatest ignorance, and it paralyzes activity, thought, and ambition. Live today well and the next step will take care of itself.

Console yourself with the thought that death happens to everybody — saint or sinner — and that therefore it must be some sort of holiday from the troublesome business of life.

— ᨒ —

When fear overpowers you, realize that nothing worse than physical death can happen to you; and if that does happen, it releases you from the object of your fears. Realize death is not a tyrant but a deliverer; it releases us from all physical pain and mental suffering. Death is the physical, mental, and spiritual anodyne [chloroform] which brings relief from all anguish for a period immediately following mortal life.

—◊◊◊—

Death is a fear to the ignorant human being, but it is a transition to a higher state to the wise — a promotion to higher grades of Life.

—◊◊◊—

Think how everybody fears death, and yet death comes only to give peace and relief when life's burden seems to be extremely heavy with grief, ill-health, or apparently incurable trouble.

—◊◊◊—

If great and small, immortality-declaring saints and trembling-at-death small men, must die, then why should you fear death? It is a universal experience through which all must pass.

FEARLESSNESS TOWARD OTHERS' OPINIONS AND CRITICISM

If we pursue the spiritual path seriously, we may find ourselves objects of ridicule to our worldly minded, erstwhile friends and acquaintances. But the prestige they would offer us is valueless and self-destructive.

Alas, some devotees foolishly regret sacrificing that prestige. Succumbing to the importunities of family members and of self-seeking friends, they return to the welcome which ignorance gladly extends to kindred ignorance. Shamed to cowardice by their sneering, imperceptive critics, they abandon their quest for God, and, hoping for the world's applause, embrace once again the fears and tremulous expectations of a life lived in delusion!

If a person sells true value for false, what can he buy to replace even a fraction of the worth he sacrificed? A million dollars in play money will not buy the equivalent of one gold coin. Devotees who, having once tasted the perfect wine of the soul, renounce it for the flat beer of a worldly existence quickly realize what a bad choice they've made. They've exchanged the sweetness of inner peace for coarse, barroom jollity, and thereby condemned themselves to a life of spiritual anguish and despair.

Fearlessness toward Disease

In a village a saint lived. He was meditating in the night, when he saw a ghost of smallpox entering the village. He said, "Stop, Mr. Ghost, go away. You cannot molest a town in which I worship God." But the ghost said, "I will take only three people according to my cosmic karmic duty." The saint unwillingly had to nod assent. The next day three died, but the day after more died, and so on, more and more, until hundreds had died. The savant, thinking of the deception played on him, meditated, and the ghost came. The saint said, "Mr. Ghost, you deceived me and did not speak the truth." But the ghost said, "By the Great Spirit, I did speak the truth to you." Then the saint said, "You promised to take only three, and you have taken hundreds." The ghost said, "I took only three, but the rest killed themselves with fear."

You must resurrect your mind from the consciousness of disease — from the thought of disease. You are reflecting invulnerable Spirit. The body rules the mind, but the mind must rule the body, and then the body will not accept suggestions of environment and suggestions of heredity. Wrong ways of physical living have been handed down to posterity. Diseases exist only when you stimulate the thought of the forefathers and thereby reinforce their ignorance. You must always remember that if the Spirit takes away the radio-active energy, then you would drop just like that. So if God takes away the energy, with all your dinners and all your society and money, you cannot live; so remember that you are living by the power of God. You must give the whole credit to God that you are directly living by His power. You do not care about difficulties — you are not afraid. Resurrect yourself from the consciousness of diseases that have been handed down by your forefathers. God never created disease. These are the truths which have been preached in India ages ago. Truth that shall make you free!

Fearlessness with Common Sense

Two ladies that I knew had a habit of leaving their car unlocked when they parked it. I once said to them, "You should take the precaution of locking your car."

"What's the matter with you?" they cried. "Where is your faith in God?"

"I have faith," I answered, "but this is not faith you are exercising. It is carelessness. Why should God protect you, when you won't do anything to protect yourselves?"

"Oh, the Lord watches over us," they assured me. "Nothing will be stolen." So they kept on leaving their car as if half locked, but half open.

Well, one day they had several thousand dollars' worth of bonds and other rare possessions in their car. They went off, leaving everything in the charge of their vaunted "faith." During their absence, thieves came and stole everything, with the exception of a minor item they'd somehow overlooked. One of the ladies lost all the money she'd been saving for years.

Later I said to them, "Why expect God to protect you if you ignore His laws of reason and common sense? Have faith, but at the same time be practical. Don't make unnecessary demands of God, nor expect Him to do everything for you just because you believe in Him. He will take care of you, but you must also do your share."

Faith must be cultivated. It cannot be achieved by mere wishful thinking. If you throw yourself off a mountaintop with the affirmation, "God will protect me," just see if He does! He expects you to use the common sense He has given you.

He will take care of you, surely, if you do your best always, act sensibly, and leave the results in His hands. Faith, however, must be watered by inner experience, like a plant. The more you actually experience the care He takes of you, the more you will come to rely on Him — not fanatically, but naturally, in the divine way.

—⟋⟋—

It is best to trust in God and not to live by fear, but at the same time you ought to be careful.

Fearlessness through Correct Diet

Animals, when killed, leave vibrations of fear, anger, and suffering in their meat, which affect the mind of the consumer . . . The vibrations of pain, fear, and anger of dying animals are retained in the meats, and so, irritating and disturbing to the equilibrium of the mind, and impede the flow of pure life-energy.

—⁓—

A recommendation for children, magnesium in food: it has a cooling effect upon a hot head, soothes the nerves, and calms the emotional strain, because of its counteracting influence upon the bodily acidity that saturates the brain.

—⁓—

To those who have a subconscious fear of inherited disease, take heart at the assurance that you need have no apprehensions as long as your body is properly chemicalized.

Redirecting the Mind through Good Books

If you are unable to dislodge the haunting fear of ill health or failure, divert your mind by turning your attention to interesting, absorbing books, or even to harmless amusements. After the mind forgets its haunting fear, let it take up the shovels of different mental devices and dig out

the causes and roots of failure and ill health from the soil of
your daily life.

—∿—

Keep your mind engaged by reading good books. This
will keep the bad habits of fear, worry, and gossip out of your
mind. Let God and His work alone reign there.

General Advice

To fear evil actions, or the influence of bad habits, is
good, and to fear to do wrong is good. Therefore, we see that
sometimes good can be bad, and bad can be good.

—∿—

Break away from religious fear, parental religious habits,
combine the best of East and West; try to discover the true
art of living, which can really daily uplift and help all people.

—∿—

From the Christian Catholics let us learn their profound devotion to God. Let us learn self-discipline from the exemplary lives of the Catholic saints. Let us omit their fear of hell. This earth can be made hotter than Hades or better than beatific paradise.

—∞—

Associate with healthy and prosperous people who do not fear sickness or failure.

—∞—

A sunny mentality contains the ultra-violet rays that kill all mental bacteria. Don't shut out these rays by a glassy look.

—∞—

Govern all the actions of your life with the honesty and fearlessness of Jesus Christ.

—∞—

Fearlessly follow Truth as you perceive it. Love family and country deeply, that through that love you may understand, love, and serve people of all nations and races. Perceive the light of God in all.

If you want real emancipation, do not waste your time. If you want to be prince of the world and conquer fear, disease, suffering, and death, do not go to bed until you make contact with God. Do not go to sleep unless you feel that He is with you. If you will do this every day, you will see such happiness come into your life that it goes beyond all understanding.

Prayer

When the cannons of uncertainties are booming,
And shells of suffering are falling
fast around me,
still I am protected in the impregnable
trench of Thy Immortal Arms.

The Lion Who Became a Sheep

A huge decrepit lioness carried an unborn baby lion in her body. As the days passed and the baby lion grew heavier within her body, she had a hard time carrying herself around in quest of prey.

No sooner would she waddle toward the small animals for food, than they would slink away. Even if the lioness tried to catch her prey in stealth, she wasn't quick enough in movement, and every time she tried to catch some prey, she failed.

Roaring with sadness, heavy with the baby lion, and pining with hunger, the lioness stalked through the forest and fell asleep beneath the shade of a grove of trees near a sheep pasture. As she was dozing, she dreamt that she saw a flock of sheep grazing, and as she tried to pounce upon one of the dream sheep, she jerked herself and woke up. So, her dream came true, for she beheld a large flock of sheep grazing right near her.

Beside herself with joy, forgetful of the baby lion she was carrying within her body, and impelled by the madness of unappeased hunger, the lioness pounced upon the flock, took hold of a young lamb, and disappeared into the depths of the jungle. The lioness did not realize that during her mad leap at the flock of sheep, due to severe exertion, she had given birth to a young baby lion.

The flock of sheep were so paralyzed with fear at the attack of the lioness that most of them had become unconscious or stupefied, and thus couldn't run away. When the lioness departed and the panic was over, the sheep woke up from their stupor and began lamenting the loss of their comrade. As the sheep were bleating out their lamentations in sheep language, they discovered to their great astonishment, the helpless baby lion crooning in their midst. One of the mother sheep of the flock took pity on the baby lion and adopted it as her own.

The young lion grew up amidst the flock of sheep. Several years passed, and lo, there, with a flock of sheep, roamed a huge lion with long mane and tail, behaving exactly like a sheep. The sheep-lion bleated instead of roaring and ate grass instead of meat. This strictly vegetarian lion had perfected himself in all the details of the weakness and meekness of a lamb.

Once, it so happened that another great, hungry lion strolled out of the nearby forest which opened into the green pasture, and, to his great delight, beheld the above-mentioned flock of sheep. Thrilled with joy, and whipped by hunger, the great lion pursued the fleeing flock of sheep, when, to his great amazement, he saw a huge, husky lion, with tail high up in the air, also fleeing at top speed ahead of the sheep.

The lion paused for a moment, scratched his head, and pondered within himself: "I can understand the sheep flying away from me, but I cannot imagine why this stalwart lion should run at sight of me. Well, this runaway lion interests me." And so, armed with determination to get to the fleeing lion, he raced hard and pounced upon the escaping lion. This sheep-lion fainted with fear. The big lion was puzzled more than ever, and then slapped the sheep-lion out of his swoon. In a hoarse voice he rebuked: "Hey, wake up. What's the matter with you? Why do you, being a brother, fly away from me?"

The sheep-lion closed his eyes and bleated out in sheep language: "Please let me go. Don't kill me. I am just a sheep brought up with yonder flock of sheep that fled away and left me."

"Ah, ha, now I see why you are bleating," and so saying, the big lion pondered a moment and a great idea flashed upon him. Then, without delay, this lion caught the sheep-lion by the mane with his mighty jaws and dragged him toward a lake at the end of the pasture land, where many animals came to quench their thirst. When the big lion reached the shore of the lake, he pushed the sheep-lion's head over the water so that it was reflected there, and began to give a violent shaking to the sheep-lion, who still had his eyes tightly closed, saying: "What's the matter with you; open your eyes and behold that you are not a sheep."

"Bleat, bleat, bleat. Please don't kill me. Let me go. I am not a lion, but only a poor meek sheep," wailed the sheep-lion.

The new big lion, beside himself with wrath, gave the sheep-lion a terrible shake, and under the impact the sheep-lion opened his eyes, and was astonished to find the reflection of his head, not a sheep's head as he expected, but a lion's head, like that of the one who was shaking him with his paw. Then the big lion said in lion language: "Look at my face and your face reflected in the water. They are the same, and look here, this face of mine roars instead of bleating. My face roars; now you must produce roars instead of bleatings."

The sheep-lion, convinced, tried to roar, but succeeded only in producing bleat-mingled roars. But under the slapping paws and exhortation of the new lion, the sheep-lion at last succeeded in roaring. Then both of the lions leaped across the pasture fields, and together they pursued the flock of sheep, and finally returned to live in the den of lions.

The above story very fittingly illustrates how most of us, though made in the all-powerful image of the Divine Lion of the Universe, yet being born and brought up in the sheepfold of mortal weakness we bleat with sickness, lack, disease, and death, instead of roaring with immortality and power, and preying on wisdom and unlimited prosperity.

The original Praecepta* teaching is the new lion who will drag you to the crystal pool of meditation and give you such a hard shaking that you will open the closed eyes of your wisdom and behold yourself as the Lion of Divinity, made in the image of the Cosmic Lion. Those of you who keep trying continuously will forget your mortal bleatings of weakness and sickness and death and will learn to roar with the power of almighty immortality.

—⁓—

* Yogananda's original correspondence course, 1938

Chapter Three

RIDDING THE MIND OF WORRY POISON

If you are suffering from mental ill health, go on a mental diet. A health-giving mental fast will clear the mind and rid it of the accumulated mental poisons resulting from a careless, faulty mental diet. First of all, learn to remove the causes of your worries without permitting them to worry you. Do not feed your mind with daily created mental poisons of fresh worries.

Worries are often the result of attempting to do too many things hurriedly. Do not "bolt" your mental duties, but thoroughly masticate them, one at a time, with the teeth of attention and saturate them with the saliva of good judgment. Thus will you avoid worry indigestion.

THE WORRY FAST

You must go on worry fasts. Three times a day shake off all worries.

At seven o'clock in the morning say to yourself, "'All my worries of the night are cast out, and from seven to eight a.m. I refuse to worry, no matter how troublesome are the duties ahead of me. I am going on a worry fast."

From twelve to one p.m., say, "I am cheerful, I will not worry."

In the evening, between six and nine o'clock, while in the company of your husband or wife or "hard-to-get-along-with" relatives or friends, mentally make a strong resolution and say, "Within these three hours I will not worry, I refuse to get vexed, even if I am nagged. No matter how tempting it is to indulge in a worry feast, I will resist the temptation. I have been very sick of worries — my heart of peace has been diseased. I have had several worry heart attacks. I must not paralyze and kill my peace-heart by shocks of worries. I am on a worry fast. I cannot afford to worry."

After you succeed in carrying out worry fasts during certain hours of the day, try doing it for a week or two weeks at a time, and then try to prevent the accumulation of worry poisons in your system, entirely.

Whenever you find yourself indulging in a worry feast, go on partial or complete worry fast for a day or a week.

Whenever you make up your mind not to worry, i.e., to go on a worry fast, stick to your resolution. You can stop worrying entirely. You can calmly solve your most difficult problems, putting forth your greatest effort, and at the same time absolutely refuse to worry. Tell your mind, "I can do only my best, no more. I am satisfied and happy that I *am* doing my best to solve my problem; there is absolutely no reason why I should worry myself to death."

When you are on a worry fast, you need not be in a negative mental state. Drink copiously of the fresh waters of peace flowing from the spring of every circumstance, vitalized by your determination to be cheerful. If you have made up your mind to be cheerful, nothing can make you unhappy.

If you do not choose to destroy your own peace of mind by accepting the suggestion of unhappy circumstances, none can make you dejected. You are concerned only with the untiring performance of right actions, and not with their results. Leave the latter to God, saying, "I have done my best under the circumstances. Therefore, I am happy."

The negative method for overcoming worry poisoning is worry fasting. There are also positive methods. One infected with the germs of worry must go on a strict mental diet. He must feast frugally, but regularly, on the society of joyful minds. Every day he must associate — if only for a little while — with "joy-infected" minds. There are some people the song of whose laughter nothing can still. Seek them out and feast with them on this most vitalizing food of joy. Continue the laughter diet for a month or two. Feast on laughter in the company of really joyful people. Digest it thoroughly by whole-heartedly masticating laughter with the teeth of your attention. Steadfastly continue your laughter diet once you have begun it, and at the end of a month or two you will see the change — your mind will be filled with sunshine. Remember, specific habits can be cultivated only by specific habit-forming actions.

—⟋⟋⟍⟍—

Concerning the courage diet: having benefited by the worry fast, try the fear fast next, going on a courage diet for certain hours, days, or weeks.

You must act spiritually in order to be spiritual.

—⟋⟋⟍⟍—

An Antidote for Fear and Worry: Relaxation

1) Physical Relaxation*

There is no greater method of relaxation than the one you are learning. Any time you are tired or worried, tense and relax your whole body; throw your breath out; remain without thought or breath for a few moments, and you will become calm.

---

* The technique of tensing and relaxing has been mentioned before. Here it is described in greater detail.

However, you must remember that when there is low tensing, tension is not removed, but when you tense *high* and then relax, you have perfect relaxation.

—ʍ—

When you tense all your body parts, you are furnishing energy to all parts of the body. When you tense and then relax all parts and throw the breath out, you have relaxed all parts of your body.

When you tense your whole body and then relax, exhaling the breath, cast away all restless thoughts. Remain without thinking as long as you can, and remain without breathing as long as you can without discomfort.

When you wake up in the morning, don't jump out of bed suddenly. Go through the routine of energizing your body while in bed.* Close your eyes. First relax all parts and then give them a breakfast of energy by tensing your whole body slowly, then relaxing. Tense and relax gradually; do not jerk.

Then get up and repeat the routine three times while on your feet. When you have learned how to concentrate, you

---

* The routine mentioned here refers to the technique of twenty body-part recharging, offered at the end of this book.

will learn how to withdraw the energy from your body in this way and turn it toward God.

2) Mental Relaxation

Mental relaxation signifies complete mental rest. You can achieve this by practicing going to sleep at will. Relax the body and think of the drowsiness you usually feel just before you fall asleep. Then try actually to reproduce that state. (Use imagination, not will, to do this.)

Most people do not relax even while they sleep. Their minds are restless; hence they dream. Therefore, conscious mental relaxation is better than relaxation which is the by-product of physical passive relaxation, or sleep. In this way you can either dream or keep dreams off your mental moving picture screen, as you choose.

No matter how busy you are, do not forget now and then to free your mind completely from worries and all duties. Just dismiss them from your mind. Remember, you were not made for them; they were made by you. Do not allow them to torture you.

When you are beset by overwhelming mental trials or worries, try to fall asleep. If you can do that, you will find, when awakening, that the mental tension is relieved and that worry has loosened its grip upon you.

Just tell yourself that even if you died, the earth would continue to follow its orbit, and business would be carried on as usual; hence, why worry? When you take yourself too seriously, death comes along to mock you and remind you of the brevity of material life and its duties.

Mental relaxation consists in the ability to free the attention at will from haunting worries over past and present difficulties, consciousness of constant duty, dread of accidents and other haunting fears, greed, passion, evil or disturbing thoughts, and attachments. Mastery in mental relaxation comes with faithful practice. It can be attained by freeing the mind of all thoughts at will and keeping the attention fixed on the peace and contentment within. By faithful practice you can divert the attention from worry to peace through meditation.

Hence, the devotee who aspires to develop uniformly and steadily in spirituality must always:

- calm the mind with the practice of concentration
- keep the breath quiet by proper breathing exercises
- preserve the vital essence by self-control and good company
- keep the body quiet and not in perpetual motion and restlessness.

3) Metaphysical (Spiritual) Relaxation

Just as there are degrees of physical relaxation, so there are degrees of mental and metaphysical relaxation. I use the term "metaphysical" to indicate those states which go beyond the physical and mental realms.

Complete metaphysical relaxation consists in freeing the entire human consciousness from its identification with the body, money, possessions, name, fame, family, country, the world, and the human race and its habits.*

Partial metaphysical relaxation consists in disengaging the attention by degrees from consciousness, subconsciousness, the semi-superconsciousness state felt after meditation, and Christ Consciousness, and identifying it completely with Cosmic Consciousness.

Complete metaphysical relaxation consists in releasing consciousness from the delusion of duality and resting the mind, keeping it identified with one's own real nature of unity in Spirit. You have hypnotized yourself into thinking that you are a limited human being, whereas in reality you are a child of God.

---

* Metaphysical relaxation is achieved through daily meditation. Yogananda's *Hong-Sau* meditation technique is taught in chapter five of this book.

A Practice of "Metaphysical Relaxation": Spreading Ripples of Peace

Fix your mind in between the eyebrows on the shoreless lake of peace. Watch the eternal circle of rippling peace around you. The more intently you watch, the more you will feel the wavelets of peace extending from your eyebrows to your forehead, from your forehead to your heart, and on to every cell in your body.

Now the ripples of peace have left the banks of your body and peace is flooding over the vast territory of your mind.

Now the flood of peace overflows the boundaries of your mind and moves on in infinite directions all around you, everywhere.

Meditate, dwell on this, and feel it.

Prayer

I care not if the shell-fire of
trials scream around me.
And I pay little heed to salvo-shots
fired in my honor.
I mind not if machine-guns of mischief
are aimed at me to riddle me:
for when Thou art with me,
I am safe behind the ramparts
of Thy protective light.

How a Saint Converted a Thief

A pious saint, Tulsidas, used to worship an image of Rama, the great epic prophet of India. Some princely devotees of Tulsidas, enraptured by his intense devotion, gave him many gold utensils to be used in connection with the sacerdotal ceremonies of his temple.

Tulsidas, while he meditated deeply on Rama, was often intuitively afraid that his gold utensils would be stolen.

His fear was not wholly unfounded, for a thief, who had learned upon reliable authority about the gold utensils in the unlocked temple of Tulsidas, every night had been secretly looking for an opportunity to steal them from the temple, but whenever the thief went to steal them he beheld the living image of the prophet Rama guarding the entrance of the temple door.

The Saint Tulsidas left the temple open, and at night he used to meditate, under a bower of fragrant flowers, about one hundred yards from the temple.

What puzzled the thief was that during the daytime there was no sentry at the temple door, yet for seven nights he beheld the prophet Rama, with bow and arrows, guarding the temple entrance. It could not be Tulsidas dressed as the prophet Rama because the thief, before he tried to enter the temple, made sure that Tulsidas was steeped in deep meditation under his favorite fragrant flower bower.

Bewildered, the thief, dressed as a gentleman, went to Tulsidas one morning and said: "Honored Sir, for seven nights I have wanted to enter your temple at night to meditate and receive a little holy vibration, but I dared not enter because I beheld your hired sentry dressed as prophet Rama, equipped with bow and arrows, menacingly guarding the temple door. I have heard that you do not lock the temple door even at night, for you always invite true devotees to meditate, I am sorry I couldn't get in."

"Is it true that you saw Rama guarding the temple door?" Tulsidas, with tears in his eyes, asked the thief who was garbed as a gentleman. "Well, gentleman, I'm sorry. I will ask my sentry not to guard the temple door anymore, so that you can enjoy your visit in the temple at any time."

The saint understood how his fear of the loss of the temple's gold utensils had caused the prophet Rama to take the trouble of materializing himself and guarding the temple treasures. Tulsidas, without telling anyone, knew that the gentlemanly garbed man was nothing but a thief. The saint retired to the temple and meditated all day long and prayed to Rama: "Lord, take away my gold utensils and desist from assuming the part of my sentry and all night sleeplessly guarding the temple utensils. I am ashamed to have bothered you with my fears." Rama appeared in a vision and acceded to the prayer of the devotee Tulsidas.

Believing in the saint's assurance of a sentry-less temple, and making sure that Tulsidas was deeply meditating, that night, under his favorite tree, as usual the thief stalked across the garden toward the temple to steal the golden utensils. There was no God guarding the temple door in the dumb stillness of the night. Tiptoe the thief softly went near the temple door and gently pushed it wide open so that he could pass through. On entering he beheld no one in the temple, so he hurriedly gathered together most of the golden utensils, put them in a gunnysack and briskly walked out of the temple. On the way out he met a stray dog who began to howl at him and chase him. The thief, with the tinkling sound of the gold on his back, being chased by the dog, increased his brisk walk into a race for safety.

Tulsidas had finished his meditation and was resting under the tree and was expecting the return of the thief, when, hearing the howl of a dog, and racing feet, and the tinkling sound of the gold utensils, went into the temple and discovered the loss of almost all of the utensils.

Tulsidas hurriedly gathered together the remaining few gold pieces, tied them in a napkin, and madly raced in the direction from which he heard the howling of the dog. Being a healthy devotee, Tulsidas ran stag-like and overtook the thief, who, in remorse, and almost beside himself with fear, fell at the feet of the saint and cried: "Gracious saint, please take back your gold utensils. I don't want them. I beg of you not to turn me over to the police, for I have a family to support."

The saint laughed merrily and, patting the thief on the back, handed him the rest of the gold utensils, saying: "Son, I did not overtake you to arrest you, but to give you the rest of the utensils which in a hurry you missed. I am glad to be relieved of them, for they distracted me from my meditation on my beloved Rama. Son, you need them more than I do, take them all with my blessing. However, I would ask that the next time you want anything from the temple, please don't steal it and poison your spiritual life, but ask me and I will willingly give it to you."

The thief was dumbfounded at the astounding, possession-aboveness, devotion, forgiveness, and generosity of Tulsidas, and held the saint's feet tightly to his bosom, loudly talking amidst sobs: "Honored saint, I am a thief by profession, but I have never seen a greater thief than you are.

Today you have stolen everything from me — my body, mind, desires, aspirations, heart, and my very soul, including the gold utensils which you gave me. I don't want to be a thief of perishable articles any longer, but I want to be a thief of souls like you, so that I may steal them for God."

Saying this, the thief, now a disciple, followed the master to the temple, and ever after they walked, dreamed, and loved God together, until their bodies dropped off like the shed skins of serpents, and their souls, renewed and quickened, were secreted away in the bosom of the rock of endlessness.

—∞—

Chapter Four

HOW TO OVERCOME STAGE FRIGHT

Stage fright is a form of fear which causes nervousness in many people, so that they are not able to do anything naturally. If you are shy and have stage fright, get your mind quiet and remember that all the power you need is within you — all the power to convince people, all the power to give the direct truth. The particular kind of truth you want to give is in the Infinite Spirit, which functions through you.

Even the dramatically mute person can learn to talk or play well by constant practice. If one thoroughly rehearses his part and meticulously remembers it, he should be able to play well on the stage. Even actors with exceptional ability feel a sort of heart-choking fright immediately before their debut on the stage. But when an actor plays a part over and over again every day for months, he feels at home on the stage and loses stage fright completely. Confidence, that you would not, you could not even dream of making a fool of yourself before an audience should bring to you that self-assurance by which you would manage to somehow act well on the stage.

The quality of your audience and the enthusiasm of your friends can be compared to good calves who pull out more milk when they are at the udder of the mother cow. The better the calf, the more milk; the better the audience, the greater the response from the actor. But sometimes diseased cows do not give any milk, so, also, defective actors cannot produce a worthwhile performance even if they have an appreciative audience. As the milk comes out more and more when the calf pulls harder at the udder, so also, an appreciative large audience brings out the best in the artist.

Causes of Stage Fright

Stage fright is caused primarily by inexperience; secondarily it is due to the lack of mastery over one's own dramatic technique, or to nervousness, or an inferiority complex.

Stage fright often arises when you are not convinced of your own ability, and when your dramatic skill is not stimulated by public appreciation. Great artists consider that half the battle is due to perfect technique; the test is won because of the confidence of the people in the ability of the artist.

Remove the causes which generate stage-fright, which are:

1) Lack of frequency in your performances.

2) Timidity.

3) Nervousness.

4) Inferiority Complex.

5) Lack of complete mastery over your technique and the

modus operandi of acting the dramatic part.

6) Over-eating before a performance.

7) Drinking or using narcotics.

How to Overcome Stage Fright

To let your stage fright get the best of you is ridiculous, for you must know that your honor before your audience you love more than your succumbing to the influence of stage fright. Even if you have stage fright while already on the stage, then conceal it or act as if you never had it, and do your best.

There are several ways of overcoming stage fright when entering upon the stage. For instance, when you are performing your part before the public, be sure to imagine that you are talking to a group of children or irresponsible adults. Failing in that, imagine that you are addressing an empty hall, and just rehearsing your act before an imaginary audience. If you practice any of the above techniques, you are bound to get some results. Success comes by grasping it and not by just waiting for it.

You must repeatedly rehearse the dramatic part that you have to play until you can play your part automatically without effort, as oil flows out of a barrel. Don't make a great deal of fuss about your acting; try to play naturally many times before your own people, at small clubs, or in private homes, or wherever there is a chance for you to display your dramatic qualifications, until perfection is reached. Then, after you gain the applause of many people, make your gig debut.

Special Exercises for Overcoming Stage Fright

Stage fright and timidity come in some degree even to the greatest artists immediately before a performance, due to protracted expectation. "At last I am going to work before the audience," one thinks. Then that feeling wears off as the artist merges his ego in the acting.

Stage fright and timidity should be supplanted by deep attention, concentration, and calmness just before appearing on the stage.

Practice the following:

1) Deep breathing: Breathe deeply a few times, concentrating at the point between the eyebrows, just before the performance. That will remove timidity and insure self-confidence.

2) Mentally rehearse very clearly how masterfully, joyously, and eagerly you are going to perform and enthrall your audience.

3) Nervousness can be removed by tensing and relaxing.

4) Take a bath two hours before, or immediately before the performance. Washing all the openings of the body parts with cold water can be substituted for a bath if time is limited.

5) Humbleness is good and magnetic and will draw kind attention and sympathy from your audience, whereas pride will cause sneers and apathy, and an inferiority complex will eke out, which will cause pity, increase disbelief, and a lack of hearty response. An inferiority complex will put a lid on your powers and prevent them manifesting and doing their duty. An inferiority complex will cause you to underestimate your real ability and will destroy whatever faculty you may possess, so down with an inferiority complex. Cool confidence in your ability, and that the outcome of your performance will be good, due to God working with you, must always keep you happy and contented just before your debut. Although you should not have stage fright, yet before your debut you must make up your mind to do the very utmost that you can do to make people appreciate your performance.

6) Get the best teacher to acquaint you with the best technique of acting, or speaking, or singing, and then, with all your inspiration and attention, master the technique as your own. Then keep on practicing your technique in rehearsals before a critical teacher, in small clubs, and so forth. Don't take criticism to heart and become discouraged. Use criticism as a stimulant to do your very best, removing all the faults in your performance for which you are criticized.

7) Eat very sparingly, say at two p.m., for an eight o'clock performance. A stomach loaded with food absorbs the full power of the attention which should be used in the performance.

As a mother carrying a child is conscious of the extra weight within her body, no matter what she does, so an artist over-gorged with food is conscious of food all through his performance, and can not do justice to his acting. Speaking, singing, or acting on a full stomach also causes indigestion; it dulls the vocal cords. The energy and mind, instead of fully working in the vocal cords, become diverted to the stomach nerves to perform the work of digestion. This is the reason why an artist should work on the stage only on a light diet or an empty stomach.

That is why even in deep meditation a food-loaded stomach interferes with the attention. In meditation, the energy and mind should be relaxed and sent toward God, and this becomes difficult when part of the energy begins to flow toward the stomach to perform digestion.

Sleeping on a full stomach is bad, for some subconscious attention and energy tries to work on the food in the stomach, and hence disturbed sleep or dream-tortured sleep is the result. In sleep, on a loaded stomach, the mind and energy want to rest and at the same time they are conscious of their duty to the food in the stomach, so the result is disturbed rest and also lack of digestion.

8) Drinking or using narcotics: this drugs the mind, the very machinery which runs the will, reason, and emotion necessary for good performances. One should be drunk with inspiration instead of intoxicants. Inspiration consciously stimulates feeling, will, reason, and all the senses to do their best willingly with the feeling of joy. Intoxicants obliterate consciousness and are disastrous to real artistic development. Inspiration is very expanding. Inspiration is a better motive force for artistic work than intellectual watchfulness and meticulous carefulness for the exact performance of the technique. One must be watchful first and then intoxicate the watchfulness with inspiration, and then perform. To such an artist stage fright is a myth.

But remember, even if you are a great artist, you must practice your technique with intelligence, inspiration, and God-intoxication every day. No matter what you do, remember that God is the flood flowing behind all the channels of your powers. Knowing this, try to feel, in whatever good work you do, that God is working through you.

—ᙏ—

Prayer

Make me feel that, though I may be in a
strong, man-made castle and clad in armor,
I am vulnerable to disease, earthquake
and accident if I am without Thee,
but that, though I walk
where bullets fly or bacteria abound,
I am protected behind the battlements of
everlasting safety if Thou art with me.

The Wishing Tree

Once upon a time there was a hermit of Hindustan named Hari, who wore the soles off his feet traveling through the rocky regions of the Himalayan Mountains in search of a certain wishing tree. The Indian legends describe this wishing tree as grown by fairies and endowed with great and trusting qualities, and specially endowed with magic powers. Such miracle-making trees are said to have been grown by divine fairies for the benefit of true hermits who might happen to seek them.

Hermit Hari was spiritual, devoted, and firm in his determinations. Long had he searched for God but had received only glimpses of Him in meditation. Next to God, the coveted object which Hermit Hari searched for was the wishing tree, which was supposed to grant the fulfillment of any or all desires to the one who sat under it.

It seemed that, although Hari had failed to commune with God at will, nevertheless he had grown great occult powers due to his austerity, self-discipline, and occasional contacts with God. It seemed that the time had at last arrived when Hermit Hari's determined search had culminated into the accumulation of good *Karma* (action). Through the magnetic power of the stored-up good Karma and latent divine power manifest in Hari, he felt that he was going to be rewarded through the possession of a wishing tree.

Hermit Hari's bud of a wish seemed to grow into a flower of fulfillment when he apparently accidentally came across a great bushy tree in the course of his travels in the interior snow-walled valleys of the Himalayas, where very few people were able to desecrate this virgin magic land with their sordid footsteps. His strange intuition at once led him to recognize at first sight that this large bushy tree was a wishing tree. Suddenly, inspired by untold delight he raced toward the tree, and standing under it as per the magic directions, he wanted to test the occult powers of this famous "wishing tree."

Hermit Hari said to himself: "If it is a wishing tree, I desire the instantaneous materialization of a mighty castle." No sooner had he expressed the wish than the great castle suddenly materialized beside the tree, spreading out over a vast area as if it had always been there.

Encouraged by the first success of his test with the wishing tree, he made another wish: "I would like to be attended by bright-eyed damsels and fairies serving me food on golden plates." This also came to pass. Encouraged still further by the instantaneous fulfillment of so many of his long-unfulfilled desires, Hermit Hari then wished for a mighty army to protect him and lo, there appeared a mighty army guarding the great castle.

After dinner, Hermit Hari retired to a secluded room on the ground floor of the castle. This room was rather dark and dreary, and as Hermit Hari lay there looking toward the open window which overlooked the forest, he sent forth another strong thought: "I am protected by an army of soldiers but the window in my room is open without bars. If a tiger comes and gets me, that will be the finish."

Just then, as Hermit Hari continued in his attitude of fear, a big tiger bolted through the open window of the castle bedroom and carried off the fear-frozen Hermit Hari. It was too late for him to realize that he was under the influence of a wishing tree which would grant both his good and his bad wishes, irrespective of whether they were actuated by good or undesirable motives. The business of a wishing tree is to grant wishes, and it was true to form, according to the strength of thought, whether negative or constructive.

My great Master often used the above story to illustrate that we all are living in this world beneath our magic-all-desire-fulfilling wishing tree of will power. Our will, being a reflection of the Almighty Divine Will, has in it the seeds of almightiness.

Most people rejoice if, as the result of a continuous will and effort in an unknown past life, they suddenly succeed in this life, but most people, by continuously misusing their will power, suddenly reap evil consequences and forget that they were created by their own wishing tree of almighty will power. It is wise to wish for good things while you are standing beneath the almighty wishing tree of your will, and be careful that you do not concentrate upon fears, failures, diseases, ignorance, and lack of God-contact. They might suddenly loom out of the unseen and cause you unending troubles.

Remember, you were born beneath the boughs of the wishing tree of high accomplishments and achievements and you must not think evil, as that will bring nothing but harm to you. Since you are under the Invisible Wishing Tree of the Divine Will in you, use it all the time to learn of God and attain Self-Realization. In this way you will forever quench the thirst of all your desires.

With blessings
Paramhansa Yogananda
Encinitas - April 3rd 1951
in the Sun.

Chapter Five

CURING THE MENTAL BACTERIA OF FEAR BY MEDITATION

Meditation is the real panacea by which you can permanently cure yourself of the daydream of matter and all its evils, and realize yourself as pure Spirit. Remember, until you have built the Temple of Silence within yourself, until you have broken down the ramparts with which environment has surrounded you, you will never see the glory of God, you will never have real peace and lasting joy. When you meet the Great One, darkness will pass away forever.

In your Temple of silence you may coax God to your altar of peace. Practice the art of silence. Only behind its portals can you find happiness and sanctuary from worries and sickness and death. Wrap yourself in your mantle of calmness and never be without it when you mingle with people in the activities of life. Hold your peace, always.

Practice the art of silence. The spiritual man, day and night, talks with the flowers, talks to real souls, and lives in the castle of his calmness, where worries and a thousand shattering worlds can never dare to break through. The tigers of worries and sickness and death are running after you and the only place that you can be safe is in silence.

—∿—

The more you are silent, the more you will find happiness. What happiness lies behind the portals of your mind no human tongue can tell, but you must convince yourself. You must meditate and create that environment. Those who meditate deeply feel a wonderful silence, which should be maintained when in the company of people. What you learn in meditation, practice in activity and conversation, and let no one dislodge your calmness. Hold on to your peace.

—∿—

When you meet people, do not become affected by their state of consciousness. When they are singing of God, be one with them, but just as soon as they show undesirable qualities, stand aloof. Meet people with silence, eat with that silence, and work with that silence. God loves that silence.

—∿—

When death comes, maintain this silence. Just say: "I am the king of immortality, sitting on the throne of Silence."

—⁓—

The power of truth is yours, and if you will make a determined effort you will no longer walk nervously in fear and uncertainty on the path of life. There is a Power which will light your way, which will bring you health, happiness, peace, and success if you will but turn toward that Light. Swim in the ocean of vastness and peace and limitless happiness beyond dreams — *within yourself*!

—⁓—

A main purpose of meditation is to quiet the heart by giving up worries and fears, and thereby controlling the life force, which works in five sense-telephones. The heart of a mouse in a mousetrap beats two hundred times more quickly than usual, because of its intense fear. The hearts of the calm Napoleon and the Duke of Wellington beat only fifty beats per minute. Children's heartbeats are much faster than those of grown people. Their restlessness is the cause. Their sense-telephones are always busy with outward stimuli. Children find it hard to quiet themselves, but when the child grows to be a man, he becomes calmer, and therefore his heart beats less frequently.

Normally, the heart pumps eighteen tons of blood a day. If you worry, you trouble the heart, and its beats become faster. In 365 days, the heart pumps 365 times eighteen tons, or 6,570 tons of blood. Just imagine the poor little overworked heart! This poor little heart cannot even rest while its owner sleeps or dreams. It is a much-abused slave. Therefore, when it has done enough, it says: "You have been a bad master, a hard taskmaster. Now I will quit my job." And then, just because the sparkplug of life, your heart, refuses to work, you have to do without the whole machinery of your body.

—∿∿—

Enter into absolute silence every morning and banish thoughts for several minutes each time. Then think of some happy incident in your life; dwell on it and visualize it; mentally go through the same pleasant experience over and over again until you forget your worries entirely. Sit quiet and meditate on the joy of silence. Think of that joy as communion with God. The more you meditate, the more you will realize that nothing else can give you that refined joy but the increasing joy of silence.

—⁓—

An important factor in overcoming karma is meditation. Every time you meditate, your karma decreases, for at that time your energy is focused in the brain and burns up the old brain cells.

After every deep meditation, you will find yourself becoming freer inside.

—⁓—

How long — how tragically long! — have habits kept you fearful about the future. If unexpected fortune and misfortune in your life confuse you, seek the only solution there is to life's endless puzzle: deep meditation, and increasing attunement with wisdom through daily contact with the ever-free, Infinite Spirit.

—⁓—

The body-identified soul allows himself to be disturbed by delusive affection, fear, and anger which arise in connection with the body. By withdrawing the mind from the body and its sensations the soul suddenly finds itself steadily united with the everlasting joy of the inner Self. Thus he finds himself disengaged from all the intimate emotions and sensations pertaining to the body.

—⁓—

A bird long accustomed to living in a cage hesitates to fly, if the door is opened. The soul, similarly, long caged in the physical body, falters when the time comes for it to leave body-consciousness.

O devotee, be fearless! Follow the wisdom-inspirations given you in these teachings.

—⁓—

In the quest for divine bliss, there lingers subconsciously in the mind a certain apprehension: the fear of bereavement, of losing one's old associations and familiar sense enjoyments; most of all, of losing one's own self-identity. Rationalizations enter the mind — perhaps the thought: "Won't God be just as pleased with me if I live a good, moral life? Must I give up everything human — everything *normal*, and be left in the end with, perhaps, — nothing?"

Be courageous! . . . Strip yourself to the quintessence of your being, if you would attain Truth Absolute. O devotee, rest not! Rest *never*! In the Absolute you will find freedom. Discover, at the heart of Nothingness, the ever-existing, ever-conscious, ever-new Bliss of Spirit — eternal release from further, compulsory incarnations.

—⬡—

Babaji assures us, however, that even a little meditation saves one from the dire fear of death and after-death states.

—⬡—

After a silence, Babaji added, "Repeat to each of your disciples this majestic promise from the Bhagavad Gita: *'Swalpamasya dharmasya, trayata mahato bhoyat'* — Even a little bit of the practice of this religion will save you from dire fears and colossal sufferings."

—⬡—

The soul that is identified with body experiences and the limitations of the consciousness within the boundaries of the physical body, is cognizant of solidity, the fragility of bones, the fear of accidents, the fear of life and death, a dependence upon experiences for increase in knowledge, and the fears of sickness, poverty, and ignorance. Every soul has to battle continuously with limitations of body-consciousness such as these.

Through meditation, the soul remembers its home in omnipresent, absolute, blissful Spirit, but after a short meditation the soul goes back again to the remembrance of the troublesome limitations of the body. Therefore, the soul, through the liquid fire of meditation repeatedly has to battle with ignorance and body-consciousness in order to wipe out the intoxicating influence of cosmic delusion and sin.

—⚋⚋—

By the *Hong-Sau* technique you can learn to experience conscious death and rise above the fear and mystery of death. You can learn to leave the body voluntarily, honorably, and gladly, and not be thrown out roughly, or be taken by surprise by death.

The *Hong-Sau* Technique of Meditation

(From Yogananda's original Praecepta Lessons)

1) Sit erect on edge of bed with feet on floor, or sit on a cushioned chair, or sit on a bed with your legs crossed, facing East, with spine straight, chest out, abdomen in, shoulder blades together, chin parallel to the ground, and up-turned, cup-shaped palms resting at the junction of the abdomen and thighs.

2) Then precede the actual practice of the *Hong-Sau* Technique with an awakening prayer, which coincides with your desire or purpose of concentration; as, for example, for wisdom, peace, and contentment, repeat the following prayer:

   "Heavenly Father, Jesus Christ, Saints of all religions, the Spirit in my body temple, Supreme Master Minds of India, Supreme Master Babaji, Great Master Lahiri Mahasaya, Master Swami Sri Yukteswar Giriji, and Guru-Preceptor, I bow to you all. Lead me from ignorance to wisdom; from restlessness to peace; from desires to contentment."

3) Inhale slowly, counting 1 to 20. Hold the breath, counting 1 to 20. Then exhale slowly, counting 1 to 20.* Repeat this 6 to 12 times. Tense the whole body, clenching the fists. Relax the whole body, throwing the breath out. Repeat 6 times.

4) Then exhale quickly, and remain without breath as long as it will stay out without discomfort, and mentally wait for the breath to come in. When the breath comes in of itself, mentally say, *HONG*, and when the breath goes out of itself, mentally say, *SAU*. Keep the eyes closed or open without winking or gazing, and gently fixed upward on the point between the eyebrows.

5) After practicing this technique deeply for ten minutes to one-half an hour, exhale slowly and completely. Blow all the breath out of the lungs which you possibly can, and enjoy the breathless state as long as you can without discomfort. Repeat three times. Then forget the breath and pray, or sit in Silence.

---

* Use a lesser count if necessary, like 8-8-8 and gradually lengthen it over time.

Follow These Instructions

Long concentration must be preceded by fifteen minutes' practice of the *Energization Exercises*.* By faithfully practicing this technique . . . and by longer meditations in the morning and at night, and also a three-hour meditation once a week, on any day suitable to you, you will find that you will be well advanced in the spiritual path.

In the morning, this *Hong-Sau* technique should be practiced after the *Energization Exercises*. You must get used to the practicing of this technique with your eyes gently concentrated upon the point between the eyebrows. Do not strain the eyes. However, if you are not used to holding the eyes in this position, practice some of the time with your eyes half open, but most of the time with eyes closed. You can practice with eyes closed, and in leisure hours lie down on your back, and watch the breath, mentally chanting *Hong-Sau*. The more you practice in your leisure hours, the greater will be the results. Work overtime and you will gain still better results.

---

* For now you may practice the twenty-part body recharging which you will find in this book. If you are interested in learning the whole set of Energization Exercises, you can find them described in detail in the Energization Exercises booklet, Crystal Clarity Publishers.

When you consciously watch the breath, what happens? The heart, the lungs, and the diaphragm gradually calm down and their muscles ultimately, during a long deep silence, refrain from constant motion. Thus, decay is stopped throughout the system, and then no more venous blood has to be pumped by the heart into the lungs. When the heart does not pump blood, the lungs do not expand any more to receive more oxygen; then you do not breathe any more. When this happens, decay is stopped entirely. When decay is stopped, you no longer are in need of new, red blood, oxygen, nor food — but can live directly from Cosmic Energy running through the medulla, and not by the energy distilled from food only.

It is always a good plan to exhale and drive away the poisons before beginning deep breathing. By practicing the inhalation and exhalation exercises, the carbon in the venous blood is burned out and partial decay is stopped in the body. You will notice that when you throw the breath out after practicing this technique for a long time and deeply, that you have no desire to breathe for a long time. You can remain longer in the breathless state than if you tried breathlessness immediately after restlessness.

BE CONSCIOUS OF INHALATION AND EXHALATION

1) In doing the above, do not force the breath in and out. Breathe naturally, only watch the course of the incoming and outgoing breath, mentally chanting *Hong* and *Sau*. If the breath naturally stops in the lungs or outside, wait until it flows again of itself.

2) Remember that the purpose of this practice is to increase naturally the intervals when the breath does not flow. If the breath goes in of itself and does not flow out immediately, wait and enjoy the state of breathlessness. When it comes out again, say *Sau*. If the breath goes out and stays out, wait and enjoy that state of breathlessness, until the breath wants to flow in again.

3) The breath is first thrown out so that you may know when to begin mentally chanting *Hong* when the breath goes in. In ordinary breathing you are not aware whether the breath is in or out.

4) Do not force the breath in and out in order to chant. Let the mental chant follow the natural desire of the breath to flow in and out.

5) Concentrate upon the intervals when the breath does not flow, without forcing this quiet breathless state.

6) By watching the breath, you metaphysically destroy the identification of the soul with the breath and the body. By watching the breath, you separate your Ego from it and know that your body exists only partially by breath.

7) By watching the breath, what happens? When you first tense and relax the outer body and throw out the breath, you have removed motion and decay from the outward muscles, but not from the internal organs — heart, lungs, diaphragm, and so on. By watching the breath, breathing becomes rhythmic and calm. Watching of the breath calms and quiets the heart. A restless and worried mind increases heart action, and a quiet mind calms the heart action. A heaving breath also increases heart action and quiet breath calms the heart. By watching the breath calmly, both the breath and the mind become calm. A calm mind and breath slow down and quiet the motion of the heart, diaphragm, and lungs.

When the motion is simultaneously removed 1) from the muscles by relaxation and by casting out the breath, 2) and from the inner organs, heart, lungs, diaphragm, and so on, then the Life Energy, which is used to pump eighteen tons of blood through the heart in twenty-four hours, retires to the spine and becomes distributed in the billions of body cells. This energy electrifies the cells and prevents their decay, making them self-sustained dry batteries. In such a state the cells do not require oxygen or food chemicals to sustain life. It is in this state that the vitalized cells do not need to repair decay, because when decay is removed from outer and inner organs the venous blood does not become impure and it does not need to be sent to the heart to be pumped into the lungs to be purified by the incoming oxygen in the breath.

This condition (prevention of the creation and increase of venous blood in the system, by doing away with outer motion and inner motion by watching the breath) does away with two things:

1) Necessity of living by the human breath.

2) The necessity of heart action.

When man can live by "the Word of God" (Cosmic Energy) and not by bread or breath, and can control the heart, his body battery will be internally charged with Cosmic Energy, and it will not need to depend upon the outer sources of life (food, liquid, and gasses).

a. This practice teaches the body cells to be bridged over with Cosmic Consciousness.

b. It destroys the slavery of the body to breath.

c. It stops decay in inner and outer organs.

d. It makes the heart action and breathing unnecessary

and insures longevity in the body-house when one
wants to remain there longer.

e. The calming of the heart switches off the energy in the
   five sense-telephones of touch, smell, taste, hearing,
   and sight, for the heart is the second switchboard of
   the senses. (The medulla is the main switch.) When
   the life-force and the consciousness are withdrawn
   from the five sense-telephones, the sensations of sight,
   hearing, smell, taste, and touch cannot reach the brain
   through the nerve-telephone wires. When sensations
   stop registering in the brain, the conceptions and asso-
   ciated ideas, resulting from them, cease. It is then that
   the mind or the attention becomes free to contem-
   plate any particular object, or God.

Chapter Six

CHANTS AND AFFIRMATIONS FOR OVERCOMING FEAR

In connection with singing, chanting, or intoning away physical disease or worry or spiritual ignorance, one must know the law of intonation from high to low, low to whisper, whisper to mental, subconscious to superconscious, chanting. This is the method of converting loud meaningful words into realized experiences — assimilating the truth of a word or words by chanting loudly and mentally until they become a part of the soul's realization. Or one must induce the superconscious, peaceful state first and from that stage chant mentally, or quietly or loudly, as he pleases.

But in all cases the intonation, whether mental or physical (that is, audible), must be injected with superconscious mentality, faith, and steadiness in the beginning or at the end, to be effective in accomplishing a specific healing. Mental chanting is best for individuals; loud chanting, ranging from low to high, or vice versa, is good in congregations.

Before chanting, the law of repetition should be understood or explained. Some Western minds often fail to grasp the changing depths of conviction in Hindu chanting and see only a monotonous repetition of a word or words. Of course, repetition of words without understanding their meaning with deep and deeper feelings and realization is useless. That is what the Bible meant by saying, "Take not the name of the Lord thy God in vain," that is, do not say, "O, God,

O, God" without attention, or while thinking of other things, or while the mind is wandering. Long intellectual prayers full of word-jugglery may satisfy the intellectually hungry, but they are only the empty noises of a victrola without the soul in them.

It is better to say just one phrase, such as "O, Father, heal me," or "I am well, for Thou art in me," extemporaneously (as it comes) repeating it vigorously from low to high, *or* from loud down to a whisper, and lastly from a whisper to mental affirmations, until one feels what one is saying. That is to say, repeating a phrase with varying depth of soul feeling until one realizes the meaning of his utterance in every fiber of his Being. This is At-one-ment with one's own affirmations through loud and mental chanting.

At the moment the phrase reaches the superconsciousness and the inner conviction, a volley of energy will shoot down and vibrate and heal the diseased tissues of the body, mind, and soul, electrocuting physical bacteria, paralyzing mental fears, and incinerating ignorance into ashes.

Three chants for overcoming fear

[Yogananda indicated the psychological and spiritual effect of many of his songs, called Cosmic Chants. The following three are specifically designed to overcome fear.]

1) When My Dream's Dream Is Done

Psychological and spiritual effect: For overcoming the fear of death and achieving ascension to God.

Lyrics:

Whence do they come here?

Wither do they flit away?

In all follies' dark sway

Keep floating on hope's way.

Take the dust of each one's feet

Serving Mother where She sleeps.

So long life sweetly smiles

Let us all swim in smiles.

When my dream's dream is done

She will lift me in Her lap.

2) *From This Sleep, Lord*

Psychological and spiritual effect: For final salvation, and overcoming fear of death.

Lyrics:

From this sleep, Lord, will You wake, wake me?
From this dream, Lord, will You wake, wake me?
In Thee I dive;
In Thee I rise, in Thy sea, in, in Thee.

From this sleep, Lord, will You wake, wake me?
From this dream, Lord, will You wake, wake me?
In Thee I'm born;
In Thee I die, to live forever in, in Thee.

3) My Soul Is Marching On

Psychological and spiritual effect: Use to banish fear, failure or discouragement.

Lyrics:
The shining stars are sunk in darkness,
The weary sun is dead at night,
The moon's soft smile doth fade anon —
But still my soul is marching on.

The grinding wheel of time has crushed
Full many a life of moon and stars
And many a brightly smiling morn--
But still my soul is marching on.

The flowers bloomed, then hid in gloom,
The bounty of the trees did cease,
Colossal men have come and gone —
But still my soul is marching on.

The aeons one by one are flying —
The arrows one by one are gone,
Dimly, slowly life is fading —
But still my soul is marching on.

Darkness, death, and failures vied —
To block my path they fiercely tried;
My fight with jealous Nature's strong —
But still my soul is marching on.

Twelve Powerful Affirmations for Overcoming Fear

1) *Divine Mother's Veil*

I will wipe the dream fears
of disease, sadness, and ignorance
from the soul's Face of Silence,
with the veil of Divine Mother's Peace.

2) *Fearlessly Toward Freedom*

I will break the shameful cords of lethargy,
and step forth in fearless freedom,
to blaze my way
through forests of limitations and delusions.

3) *I Laugh at Fears*

I laugh at all fears,
for my Protector, Father-Mother, Beloved God,
is especially attentively awake and present everywhere
with the deliberate purpose of protecting me
from the temptations of evil.

4) *Free of the Past*

I am protected behind the battlements
of my good conscience.
I have burned my past darkness.
I am interested only in today.

5) *My True Self*

I am fearless.

I am made of the substance of God.

I am a spark of the Fire.

I am an atom of the Great Fire.

I am a cell in the vast body of the Father.

I and my Father are One.

6) *God With Me*

I am protected always,

for the living God goes with me everywhere

on the altar of my ever-remembering devotion.

7) *God Through Me*

I relax and cast aside

all mental burdens,

allowing God to express through me

as perfect Peace, Love, and Wisdom.

8) *I Am a King*

I am king of myself,
not a fancy-enslaved king of possessions.
I have nothing, yet I am a king
of my own imperishable kingdom of peace.
I am no longer a slave serving
my fears of possible losses.
I have nothing to lose.
I am enthroned in perennial satisfaction.
I am a king indeed.

9) *A Child of God*

I am God's child.
I have nothing to fear
except my own wrong actions
instigated by my ignorance.

10) *Behind My Mind is God*

The eternal life of God
is now flowing through me.
I am immortal.
Behind the wave of my consciousness
is the ocean of Cosmic Consciousness.
Behind the ripple of my mind
is the ocean of God's vastness.
I am protected by Divine Mind,
which is just behind my consciousness.

11) *The Immortal Bubble of My Life*

The Ocean of Spirit has become
the little bubble of my little soul.
The bubble of my life cannot die,
whether floating in birth or disappearing in death
in the Ocean of Cosmic Consciousness,
for I am indestructible consciousness,
protected in the bosom of Spirit's immortality.

12) *I Am Strong*

I am strong, I am strength,

I am healthy, I am health,

I am successful, I am success,

I am blessed, I am bliss,

I am peaceful, I am peace,

I am Immortal, I am Immortality.

Peace, Bliss, Peace!

Prayer

When clouds of devastating war rain fire and death,
I will not forget that Thou, O God,
art my best Bomb-Shelter.
In life and death, in disease, famine,
pestilence, and poverty,
I cling to Thee who alone canst show me that,
in all dualities of life-experiences,
my soul remains unharmed.
Thou wilt ever protect me,
and make me realize that I am immortal,
untouched by the changing conditions
of childhood, youth, and age,
and of world conditions,
whether in peace or in upheaval.

*A Double Victory**

Justice, to Mukunda, was not something he could dismiss easily as "their responsibility." His compassion was too deep, and at the same time too practical, to be expressed as mere sympathy. Most people will at least weigh the risks before daring to try to right a wrong. But in Mukunda's eyes justice was a divine issue, not a human one. If he felt inwardly so inspired, he would take up a cause unhesitatingly that others, though physically stronger than he, would have shunned in fear.

Mukunda felt that the Infinite Power would sustain him against all odds. For some time Mukunda attended a school in which a certain boy, his senior by several years, took pleasure in tyrannizing the younger children. One day, as the bully was inflicting on tiny Bharatam a brutal beating, Mukunda felt a surge of righteous indignation.

Striding up to the bully (who was easily twice his size), Mukunda instructed him to leave Bharatam alone. "If you want to fight," Mukunda cried, "fight me."

The boys nearby gathered nervously around, amazed at Mukunda's courage. A slow grin spread over the bully's face.

* Told by Swami Kriyananda in the book *Stories of Mukunda.*

"Why, gladly!" he replied, sarcastically. Releasing Bharatam, he sprang at Mukunda. Lifting him up, he dashed him furiously to the ground, stunning him momentarily.

This, thought the bully, seemed as pleasant a way as any of settling their little disagreement. He stooped over and lifted Mukunda up with the idea of dashing him down once again. But this time Mukunda saw his opportunity, and quickly seized it.

With both arms he grasped the big boy around the neck, and squeezed him as hard as he could. The bully could hardly breathe. Desperately he tore at Mukunda's arms, shook him about like a doll, beat his head against the ground. Mukunda nearly lost consciousness, but still he clung tightly. At last the big boy, frantic for air, began to weaken.

"Do you give up?" Mukunda demanded between gritted teeth.

"Yes, yes!" the big boy panted at last. "I give up. Let go my throat!"

Mukunda released his hold. The boy stood up, breathing heavily. Once he had regained his breath, however, he broke his word and leapt a third time at Mukunda.

But this time the other boys cried:

"Mukunda has beaten you fairly. If you fight him this time, we'll all jump on you."

Those whose cause is unjust rarely accept unequal challenges. Grudgingly, the bully accepted his defeat.

Mukunda became a hero to his schoolmates. To protect a friend, he had beaten a boy twice his size. He might well have gloried in this victory. Later, however, when he was alone, his conscience hurt him more sorely than did his aching body. Alas! in his struggle with the bully he had neglected a much more important cause. Anger had stirred his heart. Even righteous anger, he told himself sternly, is not becoming in a devotee.

Raising his hand then and there, he made a solemn vow: "Never from this day forth, no matter what the cause, will I allow myself to be touched by anger. Hereafter, divine righteousness will be my only strength."

And from that day on, never again did he know anger. Those who knew him in later years have testified how great was his power in a just cause. But they were also amazed at the unruffled calmness in which that enormous power was rooted.

Chapter Seven

GOD: THE HIGHEST SOLUTION FOR ELIMINATING FEAR

Know that you are safe behind the battlements of God's eternal safety, even though death knocks at your door or you are rocked on the seas of suffering. His protecting rays can dispel the menacing clouds of doomsday, calm the waves of trials, and keep you safe, whether you are in a castle or on the open battlefield of life where bullets of trials are incessantly flying. Remember, without God's protection, your life, health, and prosperity are in dire peril, even though you are locked in a scientifically hygienic castle of opulence, surrounded by impregnable moats, manned by all the fire-emitting guns of man.

—⁓—

I Want to Pour the Scent of Gratefulness at Thy Feet

The doomsday clouds of inevitably tragic events thundered and poured down sheets of suffering on my life. My courage almost drowned in fear, as a million difficulties rose up to destroy me. Only by clinging fast to Thee did I survive.

Now, when the cannons of uncertainty boom before me and the shells of calumny, persecution, and fierce opposition fall rain-like around me, I am ever protected in the impregnable fortress of Thy love. I am so grateful to Thee!

When the light of good fortune dawns again, as it must always, following every hard night of struggles, it is easy to smile welcomingly at the pleasing sunrise of Thy grace. During dark nights of misfortune, however, I find it even sweeter, now, to offer Thee the flowers of my appreciation for being always there, protecting me. I offer all my gratitude at Thy feet of deep, inner communion. Receive me, my Eternal Beloved, in sacred silence.

—◊—

God helps those who help themselves and who ask Him to help them. So remember this; it is the power of God that will help you. Be fearless and feel that you are a child of God and that God shows no special favor to anyone.

—◊—

As long as you make the effort, God will never let you down.

—◊—

Isn't it much easier, really, to be good than bad? When one is bad, he is always afraid. When one is good, on the other hand, he is afraid of nothing and no one. The very gods, then, "have to watch out," as the saying is, for the Lord Himself is on his side!

—⚬—

Live with God and no fear in the world will touch you — all fears will be afraid of you!

—⚬—

Why are you afraid? Why are you doubting God? Why have fear and nervousness? Who is looking after you now, this very minute, but God? You don't know how you are living. You don't know why you are alive. So why not consciously rely on God?

Say, "Lord, my only desire is to know You."

And drop nervousness. Remain calm. Completely concentrate on Him, night and day. Say, "Lord I want nothing but you." Look for Him, eat for Him, work for Him, awaken Him in the temple of others, and keep Him awakened in your soul.

Even if you are in a fortified castle, still, death will get you there, but if you are with Him, with disease and death dancing around you, nothing can touch you."

—⁂—

Worldly consciousness is a dark, brooding land, perilous with the shadows of fear and death. When devotees enter the divine world, they pass from the gray shades of a twilight existence into the sun-filled land of Eternal Life.

—⁂—

To seek God requires a bold and adventurous spirit. Anyone who, instead, clings timidly to trivial worldly advantages and to dimly glowing earthly delights is both short-sighted and a coward. O devotee, be brave! Fear not to invest your last coin to discover the fabled treasures of your soul.

—⁂—

You fear change because you do not understand it. Your attention is upon the change instead of upon its cause. This fear is due to body consciousness. May the light of the Infinite shine forth from within you.

—⁂—

The energy of God is finer than x-rays and has the power to destroy not only physical germs but mental bacteria of evil tendencies and the soul bacteria of ignorance.

—⁂—

Realize that all power to think, to speak, and to act, comes from God, and that He is with you now guiding and inspiring you. As soon as you actually realize that, a flash of illumination will come and fear will leave you. Sometimes the power of God comes like an ocean, and surges through your Being in great boundless waves, sweeping away all obstacles.

There is a power which will light your way, which will bring you health, happiness, peace, and success if you will but turn toward the Light.

—⁂—

There are diseases which result from breaking hygienic laws and the consequent bacterial invasion.

There are maladies which result from disobeying the mental laws of Being, and the consequent attack of mental bacteria of fear, anger, worry, greed, temptation, and lack of self-control.

There are diseases which arise from the soul's ignorance.

Do not forget that ignorance is the mother of all physical, mental, and spiritual diseases. Abolish ignorance by contacting God; and forthwith body, mind, and soul will be healed of all maladies.

—m—

If you saw just one form of life, you would not see any death. There would be no death. If you place your concentration on the vast Ocean of life, you won't see that hundreds of millions of people are coming and dying. Because your attention is on the change and not on the object that is causing the change, you are deluded. When your body gets into a little trouble, then you immediately think that you are going to die. This fear of change is the cause of all trouble.

—∭—

Change does not mean annihilation. It means certain changes of motion which we, as human beings, fear and dislike. The nature of matter is change. The nature of Spirit is changelessness.

—∭—

If you can quicken your soul not to go back to the material to be governed, and to material attractions, then it can release itself into immortality. You fear change because you do not understand it. Your attention is upon the change instead of upon its Cause. This fear is due to body consciousness.

—∭—

Self-realization is just like a tender seed. You must water it with meditation and grow a hedge around it so that worries, fears, and anger will not tear down this little plant. Meditate and keep your mind constantly pointed toward the north pole of God's consciousness. Be like the compass. No matter where it is turned, the little needle of attention goes back to the north pole. And so should your consciousness. Be with

God every minute. Enjoy everything with the Infinite and you will be happy in that consciousness.

—∭—

Study Self-realization teaching in order to discover truth. You can only know about an orange after tasting it. You cannot know what it is really like by listening to a talk about it. So it is with truth. By knowing God through deep and frequent meditation, you will lose all your fears and troubles. India's Masters specialized in this immortal knowledge.

—∭—

The devotee, when he has already formed habits of material pleasure, becomes very sad when he realizes that he has to give up his very dear, long-known psychological "relatives" of evil tendencies. Then he reasons: "Why can't I enjoy material and spiritual pleasures together?" But this only amounts to wanting to enjoy a poisonous drink and also an invigorating tonic at the same time. He erroneously imagines that if he moves into the deeper regions of ecstasy, his mind will be completely unconscious of the world of the senses, and that, by continued inner contact, he may lose the five sensibilities of the senses and ultimately, through long disuse, his very sense-faculties may be utterly annihilated. The above fear is baseless, for a true devotee, in deep ecstasy of meditation, finds his sense-perceptions and senses highly sensitized by the contact of the all-powerful and all-seeing God.

—⚍—

Why did I foolishly punish myself so long with sorrow, want, fear, false ambition, worry, sickness, and ignorance, seeking Thee in matter when I could find Thy complete happiness only in myself?

I will seek Thee from now on until I find Thee. Finding Thee, I shall love to receive whatever wholesome gifts it is Thy desire to give me, though I ask nothing and prefer to be very satisfied throughout Eternity with the complete gift of Thyself.

—⚍—

Prayer

Since all things, including ourselves,
are made of Thy dreaming mind,
why dost Thou not wake up and dissolve us
into Thy fearless Blessed Being,
and melt our minds into Thy mind,
and unite our temporary joys with
Thy everlasting joys?
Unite our evading life with Thy Imperishable Life.
Blend our flickering, stale happiness
into Thy enduring ever-new Blessedness.
Make us fearless by letting us know
that we are waking and dreaming in Thee,
and that we are Thy all-protected,
ever-happy Self.

SMILE FOREVER

Smile when the roses are budding
Smile when the petals of pleasure are falling.
Smile when vigor is throbbing in your breast;
Smile when you have dreaming wrinkles
In your brow.
Smile because you find happiness in peace
And not in passing possessions.
Smile because you are fearless,
Smile because fear is ashamed to cause you
Apprehension and failure.
Smile when trials burst upon you;
Smile when the goblin of poverty stalks,
Smile when all hope threatens to leave you,
Smile when you are crying
And smile when you are laughing.
Smile when you are losing
And smile when you are winning.

Smile when you are good
And smile when you are bad.
Smile at the sad past, for it is no more;
Smile, thinking of the joy of yester-years.
Smile at the past; smile today,
Smile tomorrow, and you will qualify
To smile forever and forever.
Smile newly with the ever-new smile of God
Every second, every minute.
Smile every day in the year,
And keep smiling in God — forever.

APPENDIX

TWENTY PART BODY RECHARGING, IN FOUR PARTS

Keep your eyes closed, focusing inwardly on the energy. Apply these two principles: "Tense with will, relax and feel," and "The stronger the will, the stronger the flow of energy."

1) Stand upright. Inhale slowly, gradually tensing the whole body (low, medium, high) to the point where it vibrates. Gaze upward at the point between the eyebrows, and with concentration feel the energy flowing into the body through the medulla oblongata. Hold the tension for a few moments, and consciously fill the whole body with energy. Then exhale and slowly relax (medium, low, completely), feeling the energy as it withdraws from the body parts. Always tense with will, then relax and feel.

2) Apply the same principles (looking to the spiritual eye, feeling energy flowing from the medulla oblongata, consciously filling the body parts with cosmic energy) to the following twenty body parts. Tense with low, medium, high tension until the muscle vibrates. Then relax with medium, low tension, then complete relaxation, feeling the energy withdraw: left foot, right foot; left calf, right calf; left thigh, right thigh; left buttock, right buttock; abdomen, stomach; left forearm, right forearm; left upper arm, right upper arm; left chest, right chest; left neck, right neck; throat, back of

neck (don't tense the neck too strongly - medium tension is sufficient).

3) Now do the same recharging of all body parts, one after the other, but this time maintain a medium tension in each body part. Again, consciously charge the body with cosmic energy from the medulla oblongata. When all muscles are tensed (filled with energy), relax one muscle at a time in reverse order. In time, do the tension of all twenty parts with one long inhalation, the relaxation of the twenty parts with one long exhalation.

4) Repeat the first phase, bringing the chin to the chest.

THE HONG-SAU TECHNIQUE OF MEDITATION

As taught by Paramhansa Yogananda

Here is a simple, ancient and effective meditation technique which Yogananda taught. It is widely known in India as the *Hamsa* technique and is described in the Indian scriptures. Yogananda taught to pronounce its mantra as *"Hong-Sau."* He explains in the *Autobiography of a Yogi*: *"Ham-sa"* (pronounced *hong-sau*) are two sacred Sanskrit chant words possessing a vibratory connection with the incoming and outgoing breath. *Aham-Sa* is literally "I am He."

The sounds *Hong-Sau*, he specified, are the sounds which our own breath makes on a subtle level. The following instructions are taken from Yogananda's *Yogoda Lessons*.

You may sit on a chair, a cushion, or a meditation bench, whatever is most comfortable for you.

You can practice this technique *anytime.*

Sit erect wherever you are with the spine straight, and relax.

Close your eyes (or fix the gaze of your half-closed eyes in between the eyebrows). And with the *greatest calmness* feel your breath as *naturally* going in and coming out. As the breath goes in, move the index finger of your right hand toward the thumb, and mentally chant without moving your tongue, "*Hong.*" As the breath goes out, move the index finger away from the thumb and mentally chant "*Sau.*" (The movement of the index finger is only to differentiate inhalation from exhalation.)

Do not in any way use mental willingness or force to let your breath in or out. While practicing, take the calm attitude that you are a *silent observer* of your natural breath coming in and going out, which you are generally not conscious of.

With greatest reverence and attention practice this for at least 10 minutes. You will feel the greatest calmness in you, and by and by will realize yourself as a soul, superior to and existing independently of this material body.

Of course, you may practice longer than 10 minutes, if you feel to.

It is advisable *not* to end the practice with the technique itself. Afterwards sit in silence for a while, looking to the spiritual eye and enjoying the inner effects: maybe a sense of peace, or calmness, or joy. This is the time when intuition develops.

Then while you return to your normal life, consciously try to take the effects of meditation with you.

ABOUT THE AUTHOR

PARAMHANSA YOGANANDA

"As a bright light shining in the midst of darkness, so was Yogananda's presence in this world. Such a great soul comes on earth only rarely, when there is a real need among men."

—His Holiness the Shankaracharya of Kanchipuram

Born in 1893, Yogananda was the first yoga master of India to take up permanent residence in the West.

Yogananda arrived in America in 1920 and traveled throughout the country on what he called his "spiritual campaigns." Hundreds of thousands filled the largest halls in major cities to see the yoga master from India. Yogananda continued to lecture and write up to his passing in 1952.

Yogananda's initial impact on Western culture was truly impressive. His lasting spiritual legacy has been even greater. His *Autobiography of a Yogi*, first published in 1946, helped launch a spiritual revolution in the West. Translated into more than fifty languages, it remains a best-selling spiritual classic to this day.

Before embarking on his mission, Yogananda received this admonition from his teacher, Swami Sri Yukteswar: "The West is high in material attainments but lacking in spiritual understanding. It is God's will that you play a role in teaching mankind the value of balancing the material with an inner, spiritual life."

In addition to *Autobiography of a Yogi*, Yogananda's spiritual legacy includes music, poetry, and extensive commentaries on the Bhagavad Gita, the *Rubaiyat* of Omar Khayyam, and the Christian Bible, showing the principles of Self-realization as the unifying truth underlying all true religions. Through his teachings and his Kriya Yoga path millions of people around the world have found a new way to connect personally with God.

His mission, however, was far broader than all this. It was to help usher the whole world into Dwapara Yuga, the new Age of Energy in which we live. "Someday," Swami Kriyananda wrote, "I believe he will be seen as the *avatar* of Dwapara Yuga: the way shower for a new age."

FURTHER EXPLORATIONS

CRYSTAL CLARITY PUBLISHERS

If you enjoyed this title, Crystal Clarity Publishers invites you to deepen your spiritual life through many additional resources based on the teachings of Paramhansa Yogananda. We offer books, e-books, audiobooks, yoga and meditation videos, and a wide variety of inspirational and relaxation music composed by Swami Kriyananda.

See a listing of books below, visit our secure website for a complete online catalog, or place an order for our products.

crystalclarity.com

800.424.1055 | clarity@crystalclarity.com

1123 Goodrich Blvd. | Commerce, CA 90022

ANANDA WORLDWIDE

Crystal Clarity Publishers is the publishing house of Ananda, a world-wide spiritual movement founded by Swami Kriyananda, a direct disciple of Paramhansa Yogananda. Ananda offers resources and support for your spiritual journey through meditation instruction, webinars, online virtual community, email, and chat.

Ananda has more than 150 centers and meditation groups in over 45 countries, offering group guided meditations, classes and teacher training in meditation and yoga, and many other resources.

In addition, Ananda has developed eight residential communities in the US, Europe, and India. Spiritual communities are places where people live together in a spirit of cooperation and friendship, dedicated to a common goal. Spirituality is practiced in all areas of daily life: at school, at work, or in the home. Many Ananda communities offer internships during which one can stay and experience spiritual community firsthand.

For more information about Ananda communities or meditation groups near you, please visit ananda.org or call 530.478.7560.

THE EXPANDING LIGHT RETREAT

The Expanding Light is the largest retreat center in the world to share exclusively the teachings of Paramhansa Yogananda. Situated in the Ananda Village community near Nevada City, California, the center offers the opportunity to experience spiritual life in a contemporary ashram setting. The varied, year-round schedule of classes and programs on yoga, meditation, and spiritual practice includes Karma Yoga, personal retreat, spiritual travel, and online learning. Large groups are welcome.

The Ananda School of Yoga & Meditation offers certified yoga, yoga therapist, spiritual counselor, and meditation teacher trainings.

The teaching staff has years of experience practicing Kriya Yoga meditation and all aspects of Paramhansa Yogananda's teachings. You may come for a relaxed personal renewal, participating in ongoing activities as much or as little as you wish. The serene mountain setting, supportive staff, and delicious vegetarian meals provide an ideal environment for a truly meaningful stay, be it a brief respite or an extended spiritual vacation.

For more information, please visit expandinglight.org or call 800.346.5350.

ANANDA MEDITATION RETREAT

Set amidst seventy-two acres of beautiful meditation gardens and wild forest in Northern California's Sierra foothills, the Ananda Meditation Retreat is an ideal setting for a rejuvenating, inner experience.

The Meditation Retreat has been a place of deep meditation and sincere devotion for over fifty years. Long before that, the Native American Maidu tribe held this to be sacred land. The beauty and presence of the Divine are tangibly felt by all who visit here.

Studies show that being in nature and using techniques such as forest bathing can significantly reduce stress and blood pressure while strengthening your immune system, concentration, and level of happiness. The Meditation Retreat is the perfect place for quiet immersion in nature.

Plan a personal retreat, enjoy one of the guided retreats, or choose from a variety of programs led by the caring and joyful staff.

For more information or to place your reservation, please visit meditationretreat.org, email meditationretreat@ananda.org, or call 530.478.7557.

The WISDOM of YOGANANDA series

The Wisdom of Yogananda series features writings of Paramhansa Yogananda not available elsewhere. Presented with minimal editing, these books capture the Master's expansive and compassionate wisdom, his sense of fun, and his practical spiritual guidance. The books include writings from his earliest years in America, offering timeless wisdom in an approachable, easy-to-read format. Yogananda is a fresh and original voice and one of the most highly regarded spiritual teachers of the twentieth century.

HOW TO BE HAPPY ALL THE TIME

The Wisdom of Yogananda, volume 1

Yogananda explains everything needed to lead a happier, more fulfilling life. Topics include: looking for happiness in the right places; choosing to be happy; tools, techniques, and methods for achieving happiness; sharing happiness with others; and balancing success with happiness.

KARMA AND REINCARNATION

The Wisdom of Yogananda, volume 2

Yogananda reveals the reality of karma, death, reincarnation, and the afterlife. With clarity and simplicity, he makes the mysterious understandable: why we see a world of suffering and inequality; what happens at death and after death; the purpose of reincarnation; and how to handle the challenges we face in our lives.

HOW TO LOVE AND BE LOVED

The Wisdom of Yogananda, volume 3

Yogananda shares practical guidance and fresh insight on relationships of all types: how to cure friendship-ending habits; how to choose the right partner; the role of sex in marriage; how to conceive a spiritually oriented child; the solutions to problems that arise in marriage; and the Universal Love at the heart of all relationships.

HOW TO BE A SUCCESS

The Wisdom of Yogananda, volume 4

The Attributes of Success, Yogananda's original booklet on reaching one's goals, is included here along with his other writings on success: how to develop habits of success and eradicate habits of failure; thriving in the right job; how to build willpower and magnetism; and finding the true purpose of one's life.

HOW TO HAVE COURAGE, CALMNESS, AND CONFIDENCE

The Wisdom of Yogananda, volume 5

A master at helping people change and grow, Yogananda shows how to transform one's life: dislodge negative thoughts and depression; uproot fear and thoughts of failure; cure nervousness and systematically eliminate worry from life; and overcome anger, sorrow, oversensitivity, and a host of other troublesome emotions.

Winner of the 2011 International Book Award for Best Self-Help Title

HOW TO ACHIEVE GLOWING HEALTH AND VITALITY

The Wisdom of Yogananda, volume 6

Yogananda explains principles that promote physical health and overall well-being, mental clarity, and inspiration in one's spiritual life. He offers practical, wide-ranging, and fascinating suggestions on having more energy and living a radiantly healthy life. Readers will discover the priceless Energization Exercises for rejuvenating the body and mind, the fine art of conscious relaxation, and helpful diet tips for health and beauty.

HOW TO AWAKEN YOUR TRUE POTENTIAL

The Wisdom of Yogananda, volume 7

With compassion, humor, and deep understanding of human psychology, Yogananda offers instruction on releasing limitations to access the power of mind and heart. Discover your hidden resources and be empowered to choose a life with greater meaning, purpose, and joy.

THE MAN WHO REFUSED HEAVEN

The Wisdom of Yogananda, volume 8

Why is humor so deeply appreciated? Laughter is one of the great joys of life. Joy is fundamental to who we are. The humor in this book is taken from Yogananda's writings. Also included are experiences with the Master that demonstrate his playful spirit.

HOW TO FACE LIFE'S CHANGES

The Wisdom of Yogananda, volume 9

Changes come not to destroy us, but to help us grow in understanding and learn the lessons we must to reach our highest potential. Guided by Yogananda, tap into the changeless joy of your soul-nature, empowering you to move through life fearlessly and with an open heart. Learn to accept change as the reality of life; face change in relationships, finances, and health with gratitude; and cultivate key attitudes like fearlessness, non-attachment, and willpower.

HOW TO SPIRITUALIZE YOUR LIFE

The Wisdom of Yogananda, volume 10

Yogananda answers a wide range of questions from truth seekers, sharing his teachings and insights on how to be successful in the everyday world and in one's spiritual life. Addressing financial, physical, mental, emotional, and spiritual challenges, he explains how best to expand one's consciousness and live life to the fullest. Compiled from his articles, lessons, and handwritten letters, this tenth volume in the Wisdom of Yogananda series was written in a question-and-answer format, well suited to both individual and group study.

THE ORIGINAL 1946 UNEDITED EDITION OF YOGANANDA'S SPIRITUAL MASTERPIECE

AUTOBIOGRAPHY OF A YOGI

Paramhansa Yogananda

Autobiography of a Yogi is one of the world's most acclaimed spiritual classics, with millions of copies sold. Named one of the Best 100 Spiritual Books of the twentieth century, this book helped launch and continues to inspire a spiritual awakening throughout the Western world.

Yogananda was the first yoga master of India whose mission brought him to live and teach in the West. His firsthand account of his life experiences in India includes childhood revelations, stories of his visits to saints and masters, and long-secret teachings of yoga and self-realization that he first made available to the Western reader.

This reprint of the original 1946 edition is free from textual changes made after Yogananda's passing in 1952. This updated edition includes bonus materials: the last chapter that Yogananda wrote in 1951, also without posthumous changes, the eulogy Yogananda wrote for Gandhi, and a new foreword and afterword by Swami Kriyananda, one of Yogananda's close, direct disciples.

Also available in Spanish and Hindi from Crystal Clarity Publishers.

More about Paramhansa Yogananda

PARAMHANSA YOGANANDA

A Biography with Personal Reflections and
Reminiscences
Swami Kriyananda

Paramhansa Yogananda's life was filled with astonishing accomplishments. And yet in his classic autobiography, he wrote more about the saints he'd met than about his own spiritual attainments. Yogananda's direct disciple, Swami Kriyananda, relates the untold story of this great master and world teacher: his teenage miracles, his challenges in coming to America, his national lecture campaigns, his struggles to fulfill his world-changing mission amid incomprehension and painful betrayals, and his ultimate triumphant achievement.

Kriyananda's subtle grasp of his guru's inner nature and outward mission reveals Yogananda's many-sided greatness. Includes many never-before-published anecdotes and an insider's view of the Master's last years.

THANK YOU, MASTER

Direct Disciples Remember Paramhansa Yogananda
Hare Krishna Ghosh, Meera Ghosh, Peggy Deitz

Anyone who has read and loved *Autobiography of a Yogi* will be delighted to find this treasure of personal experiences and heartfelt remembrances of Paramhansa Yogananda by three of his direct disciples.

Stories from Yogananda's family members, Hare Krishna Ghosh and Meera Ghosh, who became disciples as teenagers, take the reader on pilgrimage to India to the sacred places and miraculous moments shared with this great yogi. The stories of Peggy Deitz transport one to Yogananda's ashram in California and his life with devotees in America.

Whether humorous or miraculous, mundane or divine, these accounts bring to life the experience of being in Yogananda's presence. They give insight into the profound love with which he guided each individual.

Firsthand experiences from close disciples are a true gift that can help us tune in to his vast nature. At the same time, these delightful stories will touch your heart and uplift your spirit.

THE NEW PATH

My Life with Paramhansa Yogananda
Swami Kriyananda

Winner of the 2010 Eric Hoffer Award for Best Self-Help/Spiritual Book
Winner of the 2010 USA Book News Award for Best Spiritual Book

The New Path is a moving revelation of one man's search for lasting happiness. After rejecting the false promises offered by modern society, J. Donald Walters found himself (much to his surprise) at the feet of Paramhansa Yogananda, asking to become his disciple. How he got there, trained with the Master, and became Swami Kriyananda make fascinating reading.

The rest of the book is the only full account of what it was like for Swami Kriyananda to live with and be a disciple of that great man of God.

Anyone hungering to learn more about Yogananda will delight in the hundreds of stories of life with a great avatar and the profound lessons they offer. This book is an ideal complement to *Autobiography of a Yogi.*

Yogananda's Words and Writings

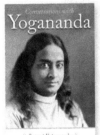

Swami Kriyananda

CONVERSATIONS WITH YOGANANDA

Recorded, compiled, and edited by his disciple
Swami Kriyananda

For those who enjoyed Paramhansa Yogananda's autobiography and long for more, this collection of conversations offers rare intimate glimpses of life with the Master as never before shared.

This is an unparalleled account of Yogananda and his teachings written by one of his foremost disciples. Swami Kriyananda was often present when Yogananda spoke privately with other close disciples, received visitors and answered their questions, and dictated and discussed his writings. He recorded the Master's words, preserving a treasure trove of wisdom that would otherwise have been lost.

These Conversations include not only Yogananda's words as he spoke them, but the added insight of a disciple who spent over fifty years attuning his consciousness to that of his guru.

The collection features nearly five hundred stories, sayings, and insights from the twentieth century's most famous master of yoga, as well as twenty-five photos — nearly all previously unreleased.

THE ESSENCE OF SELF-REALIZATION

The Wisdom of Paramhansa Yogananda
Recorded, compiled, and edited by his disciple, Swami Kriyananda

Filled with lessons, stories, and jewels of wisdom that Paramhansa Yogananda shared only with his closest disciples, this volume is an invaluable guide to the spiritual life carefully organized in twenty main topics.

Great teachers work through their students, and Yogananda was no exception. Swami Kriyananda comments, "After I'd been with him a year and a half, he began urging me to write down the things he was saying during informal conversations." Many of the three hundred sayings presented here are available nowhere else. This book and *Conversations with Yogananda* are must-reads for anyone wishing to know more about Yogananda's teachings and to absorb his wisdom.

SCIENTIFIC HEALING AFFIRMATIONS

Paramhansa Yogananda

This reprint of the original 1924 classic by Paramhansa Yogananda is a pioneering work in the fields of self-healing and self-transformation. He explains that words are crystallized thoughts and have life-changing power when spoken with conviction, concentration, willpower, and feeling. Yogananda offers far more than mere suggestions for achieving positive attitudes. He shows how to impregnate words with spiritual force to shift habitual thought patterns of the mind and create a new personal reality.

Added to this text are over fifty of Yogananda's well-loved "Short Affirmations," taken from issues of *East-West* and *Inner Culture* magazines from 1932 to 1942. This little book will be a treasured companion.

WHISPERS FROM ETERNITY

A Book of Answered Prayers
Paramhansa Yogananda
Edited by his disciple, Swami Kriyananda

Many poetic works can inspire, but few have the power to change lives. These poems and prayers have been "spiritualized" by Paramhansa Yogananda: Each has drawn a response from the Divine. Yogananda was not only a master poet whose imagery here is still as vivid and alive as when first published in 1949: He was a spiritual master, an avatar.

He encouraged his disciples to read from *Whispers from Eternity* every day, explaining that through these verses, he could guide them after his passing. But this book is not for his disciples alone. It is for spiritual aspirants of any tradition who wish to drink from this bountiful fountain of pure inspiration and wisdom.

More Selected Offerings

Wisdom Stories series
Paramhansa Yogananda
    Stories from India, volume 1
    Stories from India, volume 2
    Stories from My Life

For Starters series
    Meditation for Starters *by Swami Kriyananda*
    Intuition for Starters *by Swami Kriyananda*
    Chakras for Starters *by Savitri Simpson*
    Vegetarian Cooking for Starters *by Diksha McCord*

Secrets series
Swami Kriyananda
    Meditation and Inner Peace
    Success and Leadership
    Health and Healing
    Spiritualizing Your Daily Life

Touch of Light series
Nayaswami Jyotish and Nayaswami Devi
    Touch of Light • Touch of Joy
    Touch of Love • Touch of Peace

Affirmations for Self-Healing
Swami Kriyananda

The Art and Science of Raja Yoga
Swami Kriyananda

Art As a Hidden Message
Swami Kriyananda

AUM: The Melody of Love
Joseph Bharat Cornell

Change Your Magnetism, Change Your Life
Naidhruva Rush

Deep Nature Play
Joseph Bharat Cornell

Divine Will Healing
Mary Kretzmann

Eastern Thoughts, Western Thoughts
Swami Kriyananda

The Essential Flower Essence Handbook
Lila Devi

A Fight for Religious Freedom
Jon Parsons

The Flawless Mirror
Kamala Silva

Flow Learning
Joseph Bharat Cornell

The Four Stages of Yoga
Nischala Cryer